CU00921206

PAIN,
MY COMPANION

IRENE HOWAT

Christian Focus Publications Ltd

To Angus, Isabel, Ruth and Alison

All scripture quotations, unless otherwise
stated, are from the New International Version
published by Hodder and Stoughton.

© Irene Howat

ISBN 1 871676 42 8

Published by:
Christian Focus Publications Ltd,
Geanies House, Fearn,
Ross-shire, Scotland UK

Contents

ACKNOWLEDGMENTS

Without the assistance of others this volume would not have been written.

Dr. Roger Hurding's books have helped me greatly. Had it not been for his advice I should not have had the confidence to show anyone what I had written.

I passed my manuscript in whole or in part to a number of friends. To them I am grateful. Their comments were always constructive, even on those occasions when their advice was not taken.

Three people deserve special thanks. My minister, Rev. Alasdair Ross, knew of the project in its early stages and supported me in it. Professor Donald Macleod did the time consuming task of editing the text. Professor Douglas Macmillan provided a listening ear and was kind enough to write the foreword.

My husband Angus is my best friend and critic. I would like to thank him and our three daughters, Isabel, Ruth and Alison for their patience while I have been writing and also for their permission to give glimpses into our family life without which this book would not have made sense.

Finally, two words of explanation. Dr. Murray and Dr. Stevenson cannot be found in a medical directory. For reasons of professional anonymity their names have been changed. My gratitude to them will never change.

Each chapter begins with a quotation. Most are from the letters of the covenanter Samuel Rutherford. Others are taken from the poem, 'The Sands of Time' which is Rutherford's words written in verse form by Mrs. Cousins. Both have passed to glory long since. The poem which prefaces chapter five I wrote myself.

Irene Howat

FOREWORD

There are many forms of trouble in this world — physical, mental, emotional, spiritual; and the challenge which they invariably present to the faith of the Christian believer is so radical, that one craves passionately to be able to let in some light upon the darkness. For this reason I am delighted to recommend this book you are now holding. Written by the wife of a minister friend — both my former students — who in her own life has known years of constant pain, this is precisely what it succeeds in doing, and it does it interestingly, humanly, warmly and believably.

It is an undoubted fact of life that some people are asked to bear burdens that test the human spirit to the outer limits of endurance and it is only natural that such people and their families and friends ask the question, why? Actual physical pain is something that each of us, very naturally and rightly, shrinks from. When it becomes long-term and intense it is one of the most difficult of all things to cope with and it operates in an area where medical science, as well as pastoral care, has begun to investigate only in recent times.

The thought of pain, let alone the actual experience of it, poses a huge problem for most people and carries with it many inter-related questions. It is this problem and some of those queries that Mrs Howat explores and she does so both out of her own encounter with unremitting pain and from within the context of her Christian faith and deep, personal, experience of the grace of God in Christ Jesus.

There are factors involved in this story of one person's confrontation with pain which, while not explaining the mystery of suffering nor denying the anguish it inflicts, focus attention on the amazing truth that great suffering can not only be endured but can be redeemed. Those factors have to do with knowing God's grace and mercy in Jesus Christ, and that elimination of fear and relaxation of soul that only the forgiven can come to experience. They are handled with insight, constraint, and compassion in the story unfolded in this book.

The moral and ethical perplexity that most of us feel in the presence of suffering is, quite paradoxically, one of the strongest inward assertions we have of the existence of God. If man is just another animal in a materialistic, impersonal, and mechanistic universe — then obviously there is no real reason why these dark and dreadful things should not happen. Pain really only becomes a problem in the presence of faith. When at some crooked point in his pathway, a believer, it may be one whose faith at that moment is tortured and trembling, challenges the world's agony, the challenge is always one uttered under the consciousness of God. When the soul cries out in revolt at the pain of men, the cry is always born out of the wonder that God can permit this. That is the true mystery. The stark truth is that if you blot God out of his universe, you will still have pain, but you no longer have a mystery to assault the soul; the problem of why? has become an irrelevancy.

Irene Howat, while always writing with humility, restraint and even personal reserve, does not evade the difficult times or issues which her suffering and pain have brought. What does shine through, though, in a very unselfconscious and unpretentious fashion, is her own submission to her Saviour's will, as well as his love, and his tender mercy to her in the midst of her darkest hours. She has been helped and sustained by Christ — by her faith, her Bible and by her prayers — and, as she shares her experience with us here, we are helped as well.

J.Douglas MacMillan May 1990
Free Church College, Edinburgh

Chapter 1

AUTOBIOGRAPHICAL INTRODUCTION

Farming, fishing and coal-mining were until recently Ayrshire's main sources of income. For several generations my family has farmed and mined in Ayrshire. They may also have fished, but only with a rod and line in one of the county's many rivers!

Joe Bickerton was the son of a miner in Glen Afton. But by the time he left school he had decided that the mine was not for him. Perhaps he had watched his father and brothers go into the cage at the top of the mineshaft. Instead of the darkness and constriction and dust of the pit Joe chose to work in light, freedom and fresh air. He decided to be a farm labourer. His first job was on Drumjoan Farm near Ochiltree.

Drumjoan was run by Agnes Purdie, a widow, and her family. Her daughter Nan, who had lost her husband soon after the First World War, lived in Ayr but often visited home. Nan had three children, Agnes, Jim and Sarah, but it was for Agnes that these visits to Grandmother's came to have special interest.

Joe Bickerton and Agnes Gardner were married in 1939. The year after their marriage their first son Bill was born. But war had broken out and they only had five months to enjoy their baby before Joe was called up and found himself in the RAF. Four years were to pass with him only seeing photographs of his wife and son as he served in Egypt, Crete and Palestine. After a brief leave in 1944 Joe was away again but not for so long. They had short holidays together over the next two years. Then demobilization — at last!

I arrived on May 4th, 1947. Bill was taken a walk by his grandfather while I came into the world. When he returned and found that he had a little sister Bill went to the kitchen and laid aside some of his dinner for me! Two years after my birth Joe was born and with him the family was complete.

Mother had asthma so much of our time was spent in quiet pursuits. I have lovely memories of embroidery threads and of books. Any picture of a lady in crinoline brings back to me English country garden scenes carefully stitched long years ago. And books, how I loved books! Bill taught me to read before I went to school. The first book I read from beginning to end was "The Swiss Family Robinson." As I was just four I am sure that the enjoyment was in the achievement rather than in the story!

For as long as I can remember my right ankle has caused me discomfort. We lived right on the edge of Ayr and were surrounded by open spaces. Our walks were through a racecourse, a golf course, or along a riverside path to town. Because I found walking uncomfortable I must have seemed a very awkward child. I used every excuse to avoid going any distance — and everywhere was quite a distance away. Sadly the lovely path by the River Ayr was very rough and the one I found most uncomfortable.

AUTOBIOGRAPHICAL INTRODUCTION

My mother's mother lived with us until her death when I was nine. For the last few years of her life she needed a wheelchair. Because of this the only means of getting to town was to walk. It was then, when I was eight or nine, that I decided that discomfort or not I just had to walk. Because I had avoided the riverside until then I had its delights to discover. Armfuls of bluebells, pungent bunches of wild garlic and dainty little wood sorrels were all carried home. What they all did for my mother's asthma I can only imagine.

Perhaps the decision to walk was helped by the necessity of getting to school which was a mile and a half away. The effort was worth it. How I loved school! I have a huge store of happy memories from my days at Newton Park School. The memories of Ayr Academy are different but equally rich. There I learned to work hard and that hard work had its own rewards.

Walks beside a wheelchair had sown the seeds of a love of nature. Being a member of the Girl Guides allowed those seeds to grow and flourish. We hiked, camped, climbed, and enjoyed being young. Summers were spent outdoors and winters in the Guide Hall doing all manner of things. For me the winters were more comfortable because the floor of the hall was level. The summers were much more fun. A sore ankle was a small price to pay.

Like my mother before me I regularly escaped to one of the family farms. A kindly Latin teacher gave me a geriatric bicycle which had done war service for her. With that I had freedom and mobility with more comfort. One of my great aunts lived on a farm some ten miles from Ayr and she and her daughter made their home mine too. They were Christian folk and their influence on me has been a lasting one.

The westering sun viewed from the farm can be spectacular. I have painted many sunsets. That was my standard wedding gift during my poverty-stricken student years! One evening I was painting a sunset from the farm, with my aunt watching me work. She complimented me on it, then said something quite simple which was to begin a change in my life. She reminded me that God created a different sunset every night and that as each evening passed he changed it over and over again into new beauties.

That simple statement of God's majesty sent me searching after him. I had attended church since I became a member of the Girl Guides. I was a regular and enthusiastic member of the Bible Class. But my reason for going changed. Previously I had gone for enjoyment and a kind of fellowship I found there. From that day on I went because I needed to. I was compelled to find out more.

God worked in my heart. Months later I was staying at the farm, aged sixteen and looking for a Saviour. The love of my aunt and cousin, and their love of the Lord, drew me with an irresistible force. When I was converted I discovered that even my dear sunsets were more stunning.

"Heaven above is softer blue,
    Earth around is sweeter green;
Something lives in every hue,
    Christless eyes have never seen:
Birds with gladder songs o'erflow,
    Flowers with deeper beauties shine,
Since I know, as now I know,
    I am his, and he is mine."

George Wade Robinson

My minister nurtured my faith like a tiny plant and channelled my energies most helpfully. A quarter of a century later he still assures me of his prayers. I thank God for him and for his wife. She has suffered much pain and even in my teens I was aware of the grace with which she bore it.

But I did not live in a glistening bubble. I enjoyed school. I revelled in the adventures Guiding offered. I escaped to the farm long and often. I was a Christian and the way forward in the life of faith looked promising and good. But I had my own heartaches and heartbreaks. Everyone does.

In 1964 I left school to become a student in Glasgow. Farming and mining were not then the backgrounds from which girls went on to further education. It was decided that if I must be a student I should study domestic science. For three years I was at the Glasgow and West of Scotland College of Domestic Science. My time there was spent exploring the possibilities presented by the word "science" in the College name. I studied textile chemistry, food technology, physics, chemistry, and even became a member of the Electrical Association of Women. Cooking, sewing, home-management were all part of the course. I have been enormously grateful for them as the years have passed — much more so than I was at the time!

A year at Jordanhill College of Education followed. My memory of that is not of College but of canoeing. Somehow, I am not quite sure how, I succeeded in gaining an Instructor's Certificate from The Union of Boys' Clubs!

After four years away from home it seemed time to go back. I found a teaching post in Kilmarnock, then a peripatetic position serving various, and far separated, Ayrshire schools.

Teaching left time for reading, and reading was now to cause a pleasant redirection in my life. I used the local library a great deal and the young librarian, Angus Howat, was very helpful. When I wanted to consult some old history books in the Reference Library I found that aged though they were I was their first reader. The pages were quite uncut. By the time Angus had sliced them open for me, he had also asked me to go out a walk with him. Many walks later, we were married, in August 1971.

The first few months of married life were spent living in a delightful but dilapidated house on Ayr harbour. When we looked out we saw fishing boats. When we looked around inside we saw paintwork of pillar box red, white and royal blue. We spent a lot of time looking out of the window!

his application was accepted and our thoughts turned towards Edinburgh.

By the time the College term started that October a mountain of practicalities had been worked through. Our home was sold. A flat in Edinburgh was found and rented. The girls had started their new school. And we had begun to make friends. God was good, he had provided for us Christian neighbours on both sides of our new home.

Our first year in Edinburgh was exciting. The weeks were for work, that was understood. But Saturdays, they were for exploring museums and old closes. They were for art galleries and the Royal Mile. Saturdays were for the family. How we did enjoy them.

One of the benefits of being a student family is that the summer weeks are free. They are not free from work as College discourses, reading and preaching have to be done. But they are free of lectures and the need to be at home. During the summer of 1986 we travelled around following the trail of Angus's preaching engagements. It was a lovely time and it made up for the fragmented family life of the winter months.

In September, when the girls had settled down to a new session at school and Angus was preparing for the start of the College term, I had an accident. When I first regained consciousness I was overwhelmed with pain. I felt like pain personified. It took me time and enormous concentration to locate the source as pain seemed to be coming in waves all through me. My right ankle, that life-long source of discomfort, felt as though it had exploded.

I do have isolated vivid memories but much of the next few months has been lost in fuzziness. I have no wish to penetrate the haze or to share that part of my pain. The facts will suffice: a nerve in my ankle had been severed. The pain would lessen. By how much – only time would tell.

Months later the fog did begin to lift. The explosion of pain died down to a level which was sometimes tolerable, often not. It did not go away. Pain seemed to have come to stay, to live with me, to be some kind of tormenting companion.

Had I remained subjective about my new situation I think I should have gone out of my mind. But little by little God graciously gave me some objectivity. He allowed me to have glimpses of pain from the outside as well as feeling it from the inside. This book is the result.

Writing a book is a long and slow process and if it is at all autobiographical there is a temptation to continually update the material looking all the while for a suitable event with which to end. Today I was provided with such an event.

Our time in Edinburgh stretched to nearly five years. For the first three Angus was a student at the Free Church College and thereafter he worked in the College library. In the spring of 1990 he was appointed to be minister of Campbeltown Free Church of Scotland and this evening, Friday 15th June, Angus was ordained and inducted to that pastoral charge.

The ordination service included the singing of part of Psalm 89 and as we looked at each other during the psalm we shared a common thought. We sang the words at our wedding and now we were singing them as pastor and people were joined in another special relationship. Much has happened over our years together, much has changed, but the words we were singing are as appropriate now as they were then, nineteen years ago.

> O greatly bless'd the people are
>   the joyful sound that know;
> In brightness of thy face, O Lord
>   they ever on shall go.
> They in thy name shall all the day
>   rejoice exceedingly;
> And in thy righteousness shall they
>   exalted be on high.

Angus's ordination is an appropriate ending because it is a new beginning.

Chapter 2

PAIN – MY COMPANION

'Deep waters cross'd life's pathway,
The hedge of thorns was sharp'
Mrs Cousin

Companionship – the word has warmth, it produces within us good feelings, pleasant memories. Its connotations are positive.

A toddler's companions are chosen for him by his parents. Chosen to bring joy, fun, laughter. Chosen to encourage sharing, chosen to develop caring. An older child looks for solidarity in his companions, for a teammate. The young person's needs are different. The need for a playmate becomes a need for a bosom friend; the classmate has to be a confidant; the teammate a soul-mate. What, as adults, we look for in our companions is different again. We would list warmth and depth, sympathy and understanding, kindliness and compatibility as being among those treasures we seek in companionship.

But what is a companion? – It is someone who keeps us company. The word has warmth but sometimes the reality is cool. Companions cannot always be chosen. We can choose with whom we will spend our spare time. We can choose which congregations we will fellowship in and worship with. We can choose with whom we will climb a hill and swim in the sea. In our culture we can choose with whom we will spend our life and share our home. Some companions, however, are not chosen — the fellow student, the colleague at work, the next door neighbour, even the parents of our children's friends. We don't particularly choose them as companions and sometimes we need to make a real effort to be pleasant companions for them.

Life has other companions, and sadly not uncommon ones. For many folk among their daily companions they would have to number ill-health, or depression, or pain, or sorrow or one of numerous other unwanted intruders who arrive and refuse to go, who come and remain.

Those who walk through life with such unwelcome companionship do so reluctantly. They have no choice. They cannot opt to leave it for a time and go on holiday. They cannot even decide to have an evening alone without it. They can, however, find some solace in sharing with others who have similar experiences to their own, even in reading a book which shows that they are not isolated in their journey, that there are other travellers going along the same road.

To a lonely man a companion would undoubtedly be welcome. A man whose companion is depression or pain or illness can feel so alone. It comforts, a little, to know that there are others in the dark fog of depression; along the unfamiliar and uncertain road of ill-health; and in the twisting and turning path of pain.

I am blessed beyond words with a loving family and many dear friends but I also have that companion I long to be rid of, that unfriendly shadow on my days — the clinging, insistent,

19

demanding company of pain. In humility I share my pain with you. I offer to walk alongside you for a little on your painful journey. If you wish, I'll share some of what pain has done to me and also done for me. I'll share with you some of those treasured times when even pain has been positive, when even suffering has been redeemed.

Pain is very subjective, as everyone knows. John comes home from work with a tooth troubling him, he finds his wife Maureen has had a stressful day and as a result has a headache. The source of Maureen's stress is Lucy, their little one, who has a nasty and uncomfortable nappy rash. Each has their own pain, but none of them can measure their pain against that of the others and decide on a table of degrees of pain and dispense sympathy and graduated doses of Paracetamol appropriately. Pain is not like that. Maureen's headache is Maureen's headache and she cannot objectively compare it with the pain John is having with his tooth. She can be sympathetic, she can be practical, she can even phone the dentist, but she cannot feel it, she cannot share it. The same is true of John and his understanding of Maureen's problem. He can help to relieve the stressful situation, he can comfort Lucy, perhaps even wrap her up and take her out and let Maureen relax and be quiet, but he cannot feel his wife's headache, he cannot share his wife's pain. And little Lucy – her pain, her hurt, is hers alone. She probably does not remember that yesterday it was not quite so sore and she certainly cannot anticipate that the cream that her mother has applied so very gently will take the sting away by tomorrow. John's and Maureen's love for her does not allow them to share her discomfort and to feel her pain. Poor little Lucy.

Lucy does, however, have an advantage over our youngest daughter. Alison suffered from colitis caused by a food allergy problem. She, like Lucy, had pain, but her situation was different in that she had no red rash, no obvious sign of discomfort, she just pulled her little legs up and cried. Her pain was within her, unseen, and consequently she suffered much before the cause was found and treatment begun.

Alison and Lucy both had pain — genuine soreness. The cause of Lucy's distress was clear and dealt with speedily. Alison had a longer wait before she got help. During that waiting time we might have wondered if we just had a bad-tempered little daughter. At least one specialist suggested to us that was the case. But our doctor knew Alison and cared. She was eventually referred to a hospital, a 500 mile round trip away, where she found kindliness and understanding and eventually a diagnosis and treatment. Far from being an ill-tempered little girl she has shown great long-suffering and fortitude.

Pain comes in the two forms of which Lucy and Alison are examples. If pain is caused by a broken bone which requires to be kept in plaster, or if it is post-operative and causes the sufferer to use a walking aid, or if it is the result of a road accident or a fall on the ski slopes, the result can be seen. Family, friends and colleagues are normally very sympathetic and supportive. They rally round and help with the shopping, offer to do the driving, help with the garden, look after the children and they are encouraged as they see recovery come about. But if a person suffers for years with back pain, or has chronic arthritic pain, or, like me, a damaged nerve, they have nothing to show. They, like Alison, carry their pain within, and sadly sometimes it outlives the sympathy and the understanding of all but the best and closest of caring friends.

Lucy and Alison are also examples of another dimension of pain. Lucy's pain could reasonably be expected to pass. Even if it were troublesome off and on it would cease to be a problem when the little person outgrew nappies. Alison has to live with her problem, it does not go away. It can be treated, it is being treated, but the problem remains and the discomfort recurs. So with pain. Depending on the cause one can sometimes reasonably project its course. This does not mean that nothing is done about it, the treatment of pain is making vast strides at present. But for many people like me, pain becomes a companion which is with us all the time.

When the nerve in my ankle was damaged I hoped that the problem would be short-term but the intensity of pain which I experienced at that time was such as to make the expression 'short-term' utterly meaningless. It seemed to me then that each day was endless and each night lasted for ever. As time passed so did the period of most acute pain. But as weeks changed to months it became clear that this unwelcome guest had come to stay, that I had joined the numbers who travel through life with pain as their companion.

When that realisation developed I recognised that I had problems. Clearly I had the practical problem of coping with pain but I also had the twin problem of coming to terms with the whole concept of my belief in an infinitely good and wise God creating and sustaining a world in which suffering affected so many of his crea- tures. I tackled the two problems, the theological and the practical, and discovered that they could not be separated. It has been at those times when I have let the two become unco-ordinated that I have not coped. I knew it before, but I have rediscovered, that the practicalities of our lives as Christians are totally undergirded by our theological understanding and that theology is intensely practical.

Chapter 3

PAIN – THE PRACTICAL PROBLEMS

(Part One)

'He taketh the bairns in his arms when they come to
a deep water;
at least, when they lose ground, and are put to swim,
then his hand is under their chin.'
Samuel Rutherford

When pain is a companion, other problems often
come along for the ride. These will be different
for each person, but some will be common to
many folk. A number are obvious, e.g. sleeplessness, weariness, frustration, incapacity and
depression; others are less so, e.g. loneliness,
hurt, insecurity, anger and confusion.

The person who lives life along with pain has
to meet these attendant problems day and daily.
This can be done on a 'meet it as it comes' basis,
coping with whatever turns up. That is fine in the
short-term. When pain becomes a long-term
companion, however, it can be helpful to think
through the catalogue of daily frustrations. Like
any other unchosen companions, get to know
them, and learn to live as compatibly as possible
with them.

Sleeplessness.
The amount of sleep each person needs varies.
How much sleep one man needs will differ
according to any number of factors. If somebody

24

who regularly sleeps for eight hours a night, and who usually wakes up at 7 a.m., suddenly starts not sleeping until midnight and wakening up at 6 a.m., he might complain of sleeplessness. But how does his sleep problem compare with that of the lady who, because of back pain, does not sleep — really does not sleep? She spends the night reading, making herself cups of tea, and moving about so that she is not so stiff that she cannot move in the morning. Sleep problems are relative. The man in our example will probably still wake up refreshed, if a little annoyed, at 6 a.m. The lady will have forgotten what it feels like to be refreshed by sleep.

Since the nerve in my ankle was damaged I have suffered from sleeplessness. Pain keeps me awake. I have had periods when my medication has been strong enough to overcome pain and I have slept, and have enjoyed then the refreshment which only sleep can bring. For me, the problem is not that I lie awake, when I would prefer to be asleep; but that I am always conscious of pain when I am awake. If I do not sleep, I have no relief from that consciousness.

Sleep sets a limit on pain. If Monday's pain goes on through a sleepless night and becomes Tuesday's pain it is so much harder to bear. Sleep provides a discontinuity to pain. It enables the sufferer to lay down Monday's pain on Monday night, and to awake and shoulder afresh whatever discomfort Tuesday brings with it. It allows for the possibility of a better day starting in the morning. If I lie awake all night when does

Monday end and Tuesday begin? Do I say to myself at midnight, or at 5 a.m., 'Right, that's a new day started; forget yesterday's problems, be refreshed, start again.' I cannot convince myself into that mind-set.

God has made us creatures of rhythm. Nature has the rhythm of day and night, of seasons and years. So have we. We have been created with a rhythm that requires night to be different from day. It requires that we work for six days and rest on the seventh. We ignore this rhythm at our peril.

But how does the person who suffers from sleeplessness maintain the rhythm of night and day? In the normal course of events our days are active and our nights are passive. For the person who has constant pain there is a real danger that these can become reversed. If the person is handicapped by pain, or if their pain is a result of handicap, they may be relatively inactive during the day, and then toss and turn all night.

At one point I found that my days and nights were becoming alarmingly alike. When I had not slept for some nights I could, especially just about dawn, be quite disoriented. Because my problem by then was clearly becoming long-term it was important to work this problem out. If I tossed and turned all night Angus had no sleep either. Because the night is long and lonely without sleep we would lie and talk. Angus struggled to stay awake because he knew that pain prevented me sleeping. Only when I got no reply would I realise just how exhausted this pattern was causing him to be. I could rest during the day but Angus could not. Something had to be done.

It seemed to me that I should make my nights as passive as possible to maintain my God-determined rhythm. I now have activities which I will engage in only during the night, activities which are quite legitimate for daytime but which for me have become alternatives to sleep. I used to listen to the radio while I worked around the house. I enjoyed it a lot. I rarely have the radio on during the day, that is a night activity. What a blessing the World Service of the BBC has been to me, and the availability of earphones has been to Angus! It begins transmitting around 12.45 a.m. and ends just before 6 a.m., so coinciding perfectly with a sleepless night.

I have a small collection of favourite cassettes which I keep beside the bed. They are my most special tapes and, like the radio, I no longer listen to any of them during daylight hours. This means that I can, around 2.30 a.m., find myself enjoying the end of a radio play, and genuinely looking forward to listening to a tape when it finishes.

All of this requires that I am fairly relaxed during the night, that I don't spend the time being frustrated because I am awake. There are times when I do feel like that – they are bad patches. One thing which has helped enormously in this respect is another cassette. When I was in hospital for rehabilitation I was introduced to the benefits of relaxation techniques.

Being able to deeply relax muscles reduces tension and helps relieve pain. I was given a relaxation cassette which had been made by one of the psychologists on the staff. This talks me through a process of physical and mental relaxation and has been very beneficial.

A temptation during a wakeful night is to get up and wander about, perhaps make tea, or switch on the fire and read a book. Thirst is a real problem in a long night. Some medication causes this to be a particular nuisance. When I find this to be the case I leave a drink beside the bed rather than get up and embark on a 'day-type activity.' Books I avoid, I read during the evenings.

When days lack beginning and end it becomes well-nigh impossible to obey Christ's instruction in Matthew 6:34, 'Do not worry about tomorrow, for tomorrow will worry about itself. Each day has enough trouble of its own.' If care is taken to keep night and day distinct it becomes easier to live in the light of God's promise, 'My grace is sufficient for you, for my power is made perfect in weakness' (2 Cor. 12:9). We are probably at our very weakest in the middle of a night disturbed by pain or illness or depression. But even at that time of great vulnerability we have the promise that God's grace is sufficient.

Does this all sound like a counsel of perfection? I hope not. While I do enjoy a good play, or a favourite tape, during the night I still would prefer to sleep. After a number of nights of wakefulness I long for sleep. I long for the release it gives from pain, for the break from the loneliness of the night, for the sheer oblivion. But, if for the present, sleeplessness is a problem, I have no choice but to come to terms with it as best I can.

Night can be a lonely time. But there is One who is always awake, always near, 'He who watches over you will not slumber; indeed, he who watches over Israel will neither slumber or sleep. The Lord watches over you, the Lord is your shade at your right hand; the sun will not harm you by day, nor the moon by night' (Ps. 121:3-5).

David, the psalmist, sometimes was wakeful. 'On my bed I remember you; I think of you through the watches of the night. Because you are my help, I sing in the shadow of your wings. My soul clings to you; your right hand upholds me' (Ps. 63:6-8).

Awake, we may feel lonely, but Scripture assures us we are never alone.

Weariness.
Sleepless nights result in a great weariness. But, even if sleep relieves pain and refreshes the sufferer, pain itself is enormously tiring. Any companion who clings, who demands attention, who refuses to go away, is draining. Living with pain is like spending time with a perpetually whining child. Most folk know how tiring that is!

I spent some months in a wheelchair. Manoeuvring a wheelchair can be fun. For a time the greatest treat my daughters' friends could have when they came to play was a time in my wheelchair. But they could get out of it and play tennis. These months coincided with a period of sleeplessness. I was physically tired. My arms and hands longed for a break from being my means of propulsion. My mind ached for emptiness. As the weeks passed I did less and less of things I enjoyed becaused the necessities of life took ever longer to achieve.

In the morning I felt I had to do as much in the house as I could because I was never sure when my energy would flag. By the evening my arms rebelled against holding a book and my eyes did not want to focus. I would leave my quiet time until late so that my energy was well-used. By the time 'later' came my Bible felt so heavy and my mind was befuddled. I had fallen into one of Satan's best used traps. It took some time before I realised where I was, and longer still before I got out of it. It was a wise saint who recognised that on a busy day he had to spend even longer of the morning in prayer.

Jesus, during his earthly ministry, was constantly finding himself surrounded by whining folk. They came complaining about ill-health, moaning about their problems, even grousing when he carried out compassionate acts of healing. Jesus, who was fully God, was also fully man. He knew and experienced weariness. He knew what it was to need a break. He identified with his disciples in their tiredness. 'Because so many people were coming and going that they did not even have a chance to eat, he (Jesus) said to them, "Come with me by yourselves to a quiet place and get some rest"' (Mark 6:31). Jesus felt the weariness which comes from constant, draining companionship.

Jesus must also have known the weariness that comes from suffering. Think of Gethsemane. There our Lord was 'sorrowful and troubled', he said to his disciples, 'My soul is overwhelmed with sorrow to the point of death. Stay here and keep watch with me' (Matt. 26:37-38). He wrestled in prayer with his Father while his friends slept. We cannot enter into the depth of heaviness Christ must have endured there. But his experience then assures us that he, the Son of God, can and does enter into the feelings of our weariness. He remembers what it felt like.

Not only does the reigning Lord remember the weariness of suffering, he also remembers the weight of pain. For our sake he paid the price of our salvation. He paid the wages of sin. He died. What the Lord endured on the cross we cannot begin to imagine. He plumbed the depths of human agony. He must also have dragged the deep sea of human exhaustion.

Is there anything we can learn from our Lord's life which will help us to cope with weariness? Two things stand out from the gospel record. Firstly, Christ knew the need to go to a 'quiet place and rest awhile'. When weariness is a long-term problem we do ourselves a disservice to attempt an action-packed life. It becomes a necessity to look at our activities carefully and work out our priorities regarding them. This is not easy. Many Christians would see relaxation and resting not as necessities but as a self-indulgence.

Jesus tells us, 'Love your neighbour as you love yourself' (Mark 12:31). Believers are very conscious of loving their neighbour but especially the weary Christian must be sure to love himself enough. Secondly, when Christ experienced the trauma of Gethsemane he took some friends with him. They fell asleep, they let him down, but he wanted them there. Friends are gifts from God and, like God's other gifts, we should use them. The Bible tells us to, 'Carry each other's burdens, and in this way you will fulfil the law of Christ' (Gal. 6:2). Rest, relaxation, friendship and fellowship, they are all fine restoratives, especially in times of weariness. They are sanctioned by no less an example than Jesus Christ.

Frustration.

When the simplest task becomes an enormous obstacle; when the mundane becomes the impossible; when the expected cannot be achieved, feelings of frustration well up in even the calmest of individuals. Frustration comes to us in two ways. The first is easier – that is when something occurs out of the blue and we find we cannot cope with it. The second is more of a problem – when we begin to anticipate situations where we will experience frustration.

An example of the first happened to me in the

early hours of one morning. Ruth, our middle daughter, was sick. That was not too much of a problem for her, she cuddled back down to sleep. I suddenly discovered that I had no way of getting the bowl to the bathroom. I could not hold it and negotiate the hall in my wheelchair. I could not carry it and use my crutches! I had no alternative but to get down on my hands and knees and somehow get it there by that means. As I passed the door of the bedroom where the other girls were sleeping, Isabel roused and was met by the sight of her mother crawling past the door pushing a bowl in the direction of the bathroom! The minutes before I worked out how to get there was a time of extreme frustration. It was a 'laugh or cry' situation. Because Isabel woke up and saw me, we laughed. I was grateful for that. I think I might have cried otherwise.

Family holidays are my best example of the second. Everyone looks forward to going away together. We pack carefully. We plan the journey. We anticipate seeing old friends again. All of this we do together. But I have other feelings of anticipation: of keeping the family back when they want to be out walking or climbing a hill; of sitting reading a book when I long to be skimming stones in the river with them. In fact, I find myself anticipating frustration. Consequently, even before we have caught the train, I am experiencing frustration.

The first kind of frustration is an immediate reaction to an unforeseen situation. The second is quite another; the second, as far as I am concerned, is sinful self-indulgence.

Frustration, as an immediate reaction, has to be dealt with immediately. It can be done by pushing the bowl to the bathroom, or whatever is the equivalent physical contortion. Or time can be spent by looking at the difficult situation objectively, deciding that it is outside of present limitations, and being humble enough to ask for help.

Anticipating frustration is altogether different. To project forward and to decide to react negatively to what has yet to happen is sinful. It is sinful because it is to deny that God's grace is sufficient. It is tantamount to saying that tomorrow is not in God's hands, even if we grudgingly allow that today has been. But Jesus tells us to live in our todays not our tomorrows, 'Do not worry about tomorrow, for tomorrow will worry about itself. Each day has enough trouble of its own' (Matt. 6:34).

James, in his epistle, has something to say about folk who boast about what they are going to do tomorrow. It applies exactly to anticipating tomorrow's frustration, because to do that is to boast that my tomorrow is going to be too big a problem for God's grace. James says, 'Why, you do not even know what will happen tomorrow. What is your life? You are a mist that appears for a little while and then vanishes. Instead you ought to say, "If it is the Lord's will, we will live and do this or that."' (4:14–15). This is a lesson I need to learn and relearn regularly.

Incapacity.

Coping with incapacity is two-pronged. It is a process of acceptance and it is a life of practice. I am using the word incapacity to describe a limiting condition in which someone finds himself and about which he is unable to do anything.

The man who has had a stroke and has lost the use of his right side may struggle and rage but that will not move the muscles of his right arm. He has the choice either he goes through his days fretting about his arm and letting that negative approach colour his whole outlook, or alternatively he can work at coming to terms with his handicap and so live in reasonable relationship with life. A balance has to be found here. It is the balance which prevents self-martyrdom.

A student who has been studying too hard and has a headache does not think to himself that he must just accept it as his lot. He has a break, a walk in the fresh air, and something to take away the discomfort. So with any pain or incapacity caused by pain. We must explore all the avenues of relief and get all the practical help we can. But in the end of the day there has to come a time of acceptance, especially for the Christian.

Paul found himself in some dreadful situations: in prison, in chains, away from most of his friends, and suffering from whatever was his 'thorn in the flesh'. How did he react? 'I have learned to be content whatever the circumstances. I know what it is to be in need, and I know what it is to have plenty. I have learned the secret of being content in any and every situation, whether well fed or hungry, whether living in plenty or in want. I can do everything through him who gives me strength' (Phil. 4:11-13). The secret of Paul's acceptance was his faith in the God who gave him strength. I am so glad that Paul used the word 'learn.' It shows that there was real effort involved and that it was not a process which took only a moment.

Living with incapacity is not only a spiritual exercise, it is also a practical, physical one. I am as God made me. Even my incapacity is in some way to his glory. I cannot understand this now, although I hope I will in heaven. But I can make every effort to glorify God in my life despite my physical limitations.

The person with a handicap has to learn to define his handicap. In my case I had used a caliper for support for some time but that did not cause a vast problem. However a damaged nerve resulted for a while in my being in a wheelchair, and I can now get about using crutches. I have attended physiotherapy and hydrotherapy to try to increase my mobility. Even though at times my progress has seemed to be slow, I have continued to make use of whatever means can be of help to me. I have, over the years, had to look at my disability, to examine my handicap to be sure that I was not at any time rendering myself less able, or pretending to be more able, than I was. Sometimes I have got it wrong. Before I had a nerve problem I would take a bus along the road

to shop. When I progressed out of my wheelchair to using crutches I walked instead of
catching a bus! I am still not quite sure what I
was trying to prove!

During the time I was in rehabilitation hospital
I learned something important which related to
this problem. I quote from my diary, written the
day I was discharged: 'When I needed my caliper
I saw myself as a normal person who happened
to need spectacles and a caliper. Over the last
couple of years, I think, because of the degree of
pain, my thinking has changed. I perceived
myself, although I didn't realise it until now, as a
handicapped person who struggled to be super-
human. As a result I constantly failed.' I failed
because I was setting myself unattainable aims. I
was trying to be what, for the time being and in
the providence of God, I was unable to be.

Depression.

In the natural course of life we all have our ups
and downs. Most of us, at some time, would say
we were feeling a bit depressed, yet not all of us
suffer from depression. A low, which is deep
enough to be recognised and treated as depression, is quite a different thing from the
average person feeling 'pretty fed up'.

A dictionary definition of depression is, 'a
lowering in quality, vigour, value, a reduction in
activity; a lowering of pitch.' According to that
definition, living with pain is a depressing experience. It seems to lower the quality of life. It
certainly reduces vigour. It can make the sufferer

feel of little value. It does reduce activity. The whole tone or pitch of living indeed seems to be lowered.

It often comes as no surprise to those who care for a person in pain that he should suffer from a time or times of depression. It sometimes comes as a great shock to the person himself. He is so involved with coping, he tries to be so practical and matter of fact, that he considers his body too much and his mind too little. But God made us — body, soul and spirit — a unity. Each part of us is entirely bound up with the rest of us. We cannot divide ourselves and expect our bodily situation not to affect our mental attitude. The Christian must be especially careful to remember that his bodily and mental health also affect his spiritual well-being.

When a time of depression comes upon a Christian in pain, the devil tries to work his worst. He can assault the sufferer with doubts and fears. He makes him wonder what he has done to deserve his pain. He can cause him to question God's love. Satan fills him with lack of assurance, feeds him on thoughts that Christians ought not to suffer from depression; and tries to take away his joy and peace in believing.

The person living with pain is already carrying a heavy load. If that becomes even weightier with the added burden of depression, the Christian sufferer is well advised to share it. We are not made to bear such burdens alone. Jesus holds out his hands to the heavy-laden, 'Come to me, all you who are weary and burdened, and I will give you rest' (Matt. 11:28). Christians ought also to copy their Master, 'Carry each other's burdens, and this way you will fulfil the law of Christ' (Gal. 6:2). God also and often works through medical means, and an understanding and concerned family doctor is quite literally a 'God-send'.

Over my time of pain and disability I have had patches of being down. I have been greatly blessed in that a few Christian friends allowed me to share my bad times with them. They did not need to come and say to me, 'Irene, do you want to talk?' They cared in practical ways and made themselves available so that I could talk to them. Lorraine would hand in a meal which meant I would have time to sit down and chat to her if I chose. Rosemary regularly invited me for an hour in the evening when all the children were in bed. It is not possible to talk at much depth with little children needing attention, or older children trying to listen to the conversation.

Friends were able to help because they did not push their help on me. They were able to support in the bad patches because they were rejoicing with us in the good times. I have heard of 'fair weather friends', folk who melt away when anything goes wrong. I discovered that there are also 'foul weather friends', people who come rushing when things go wrong. They do an enormous amount of practical help. Sometimes they also try to help at a deep and emotional level. But they have *not* won that right. That is the place of the friend who is there regardless of the weather today or the forecast for tomorrow.

My doctor has been caring and compassionate in the extreme. I owe him a debt I will never be able to repay.

For some months my pain was such that I required to take a very potent cocktail of drugs. When the time came to stop taking them, despite being weaned off them very gently, I had a dreadful period of withdrawal. Towards the end of that time I wakened up one morning feeling fine, then saw and felt a dull grey cloud settling on me. I discovered that day the meaning of depression. Thankfully my family doctor realised what was happening, and prescribed suitable medication. Within a very few weeks the cloud lifted. It was so relieving to be able to praise God again from my heart; over those weeks I had lived like the psalmist, in anticipation, 'Why are you cast down, O my soul? Why are you so disturbed within me? Put your hope in God, FOR I WILL YET PRAISE HIM, my Saviour and my God' (Ps. 43:5).

Sleeplessness, weariness, frustration, incapacity and depression — some or all of these are often the experience of the person in pain. They are not there all the time, thank God, but they companion him through life. Most people realise that they might be problems and are understanding.

Chapter 4

PAIN – THE PRACTICAL PROBLEMS

(Part Two)

'Aye my murkiest storm-cloud
Was by a rainbow spann'd.'
Mrs Cousin

We have been thinking of some of the difficulties
that come along with pain, and the ones we have
thought of so far are just what one might expect.
However, there are other, more unexpected, feelings spawned by living with pain. Less obvious
they may be, more easy to cope with they are not. A
life lived with pain can be a life marred by
loneliness, dulled by hurt, threatened by insecurity,
assaulted by anger, and adrift with confusion.
Mercifully, no life is always plagued by negative
experiences, and when it is, it is not subject to the
whole catalogue. That would be intolerable. But
from time to time they do arise, so, like pain's other
companions, let us get to know them.

Loneliness.
At the beginning of our thinking on the subject
of pain we recognised that no one person can
feel or experience the pain of another. Pain is
totally subjective. For all our gifts of communi-
cation we cannot describe pain in such a way
that the person with whom we are sharing can
feel what we are feeling. We experience our pain
alone. There is a fine line, and a short space of

time, between a situation we must face alone, and feelings of loneliness. Those times when I have found the going toughest have been the times I have felt most on my own. I remember so well the relief of sharing how alone I felt with a friend who is a doctor, and finding that he was not surprised because he had heard it before from others in similar situations. That did not make me feel less lonely, but it did make me feel more normal.

By its very nature we cannot communicate our pain. This has two effects. Firstly, we feel frustrated in our effort to share our experience with those close to us, because we know we are failing fully to do so and, secondly, our nearest and dearest feel unable to understand and impotent to help.

What do we do in the face of this very real dilemma? Some talk their way round the whole circle of their friends just hoping that someone, somewhere, will understand. Others, in the face of the impossibility of the task, give up sharing at depth, and so cut themselves off from the support that is available, and close the door on those who are lovingly trying to help. Yet others do a mixture of the two, they keep their own feelings to themselves until they can do so no longer, then the floodgates open and family and friends are startled to discover the extent of pain and upset of which they were unaware.

However, what we are thinking about here is not pain but the loneliness which sometimes comes along with it. It is so very easy to become muddle-minded when things are hard, and to

make matters even worse we cannot communicate our pain. But that does not mean that we
cannot share the loneliness caused by it. The
one we bear alone by necessity, the other by
choice.

Prior to his crucifixion, at no point in his
earthly life must Jesus have felt so alone as he
did in Gethsemane. He was in anguish, knowing
only too clearly what the following few hours
would hold: pain, torture, horror, indescribable
degradation. Jesus Christ could share nothing of
his pain. He had to bear that alone. He was the
Son of God, but he was a man through and
through.

His pain produced in him what my pain
produces in me. The almighty, incarnate, Son of
God was lonely. We see him walking towards
Gethsemane with his disciples, and particularly
and specifically asking three of them to keep him
company. He, the Lord of heaven and earth, was
in agony and needed the closeness of his friends.
Jesus said to them, 'My soul is overwhelmed with
sorrow to the point of death. Stay here and keep
watch with me' (Matt. 26:38).

We can learn two things from that most
moving of insights into the heart of Jesus. Firstly,
God understands. Jesus Christ, the Lamb in the
midst of the throne in heaven, understands. He
understands because he remembers. He knows
what I feel like in my loneliness because he
remembers what he felt in his. Jesus' understanding is not academic, nor is it only that
gained from his being the Creator of his creatures

and therefore perfectly comprehending how they function. His understanding is complete, and from his own personal experience. 'We have not a high priest which cannot be touched with the feeling of our infirmities; but was in all points tempted like as we are, yet without sin' (Heb. 4:15 (AV)). The verse which follows sends us to the first refuge of the lonely Christian — 'Let us then approach the throne of grace with confidence, so that we may receive mercy to help in the time of our need.'

Secondly, we should follow the Lord's example: in his loneliness he sought out the company of his friends. A real friend will not only be there when the news is good, when the sun is shining, and all is well. Those friends who make themselves available when the going is hard know what they are doing. They know that they are offering to keep us company along a rough road. If, as we go, we prattle on about inanities they will feel unused. We must accept their offer, and allow their companionship to percolate to the dark and lonely corners of our hearts.

Some time ago I shared a little of my feelings of loneliness, by letter (it's easier to admit weakness in a letter!), with two friends in Finland. Matti phoned in reply, and in the course of the conversation said something I will never forget. 'Please, Irene,' he said, 'please allow me the privilege of helping to bear your burden.' Matti was right. It is a high privilege to bear another's burden. Despite the cost of his call from Finland

Matti encouraged me to talk and was unhurried and tender in his responses. When we share our loneliness and our weakness with a friend, we pay them an enormous compliment.

Possibly the hardest person to admit loneliness to, is the one to whom we are closest. It seems almost a ridiculous statement to make to a loving and attentive husband – 'I feel lonely'. It sounds crazy, in our home full of three growing girls, to admit it – 'I feel lonely'.

The very closeness of my relationship with Angus made telling him of my loneliness more difficult. I used this manuscript in its embryonic form to work out my own thoughts. Such was the embarrassment my loneliness caused me that my way of telling him about it was to let him read a word processed print-out of my writing! Angus understood. I knew he would understand. It was I who did not understand my loneliness.

But to admit it is to begin to dispel it. To harbour it is to let it breed. In the midst of a busy life, when pain is pressing, to admit the need of friends, is to confess to weakness – the same weakness as Jesus knew.

Hurt.
When I was admitted to our local rehabilitation hospital for treatment I was suffering from, shall we say, x degrees of pain. I was discharged three weeks later still experiencing x degrees of pain but feeling much relieved. Had I been able to share my pain in the rarefied atmosphere of the hospital? No, even there pain has to be borne alone.

Had I been helped to sleep, long and soundly, so becoming better able to bear the pain the days brought? No, I rarely slept. I drank much tea, listened for hours to music, and thought many thoughts, during the long dark hours. Had it been a contented and leisurely time, free of the responsibilities of home and family? No, it was an enormously difficult time, and full of physically hard work. So what made the difference?

The difference was that I was discharged with only x degrees of pain, whereas I had been admitted with the same pain, plus a lot of hurt. I needed the time there, and the help I received there, to separate my hurt from my pain. Having separated the two, I discovered that I could share and lessen my hurts, and so much reduce the total burden I was carrying. I cannot make this process sound easy – it was for me incredibly difficult.

Over the years I have been privileged to share the problems and concerns of a few folk. Without consciously thinking about it I made an assumption about myself (an assumption that was quite wrong), that, as I was sometimes able to share another's hurts, I must be strong enough to carry my own. What pride! I justified my feelings by admitting that my strength came from God, but really I saw myself as emotionally quite strong. What pride! That pride cost me dearly. When the going got tough for me I did not find it easy to talk, as I had let others talk to me. I did not find it easy to cry, as I had encouraged others to do. I did not find it easy to share my hurt feelings, as I had allowed others to do. I could justify this too — God was upholding me. But I did not even admit my hurts to him.

During my time in hospital my senior registrar was a Christian. One day he asked me how, in my situation, I perceived Jesus. I thought about it, and answered, true to character. I saw Jesus strengthening me, supporting me, enabling me. He agreed that indeed he was doing all of these things, but asked me to try to think for a while a little differently. He asked me to try to see Jesus, with his arm around me, crying with me, sharing my hurt. That insight allowed a quantum leap in my approach to my own situation. It legitimised my buried feelings of sadness and grief. It allowed me to admit hurt. It enabled me to feel weak. It let me cry.

I had been so busy, for so long, appearing to cope so well. Underneath there was hurt I had not allowed myself to recognise, far less express. I had never admitted, even to myself, that I felt sad at losing my ability to walk. I had not stopped 'coping' long enough to feel. During my stay in hospital, I was stopped, and I felt — I felt as I had never felt before. I was startled and discomforted by the intensity of my feelings. I did not know I could feel so sad. I was thrown by such feelings of weakness as I had never previously known. I was taken aback by the spectacle of my own hurt.

The rehabilitation team in hospital helped me to explore my hurt and, bit by bit, to admit it, to think it through, to share it. I even discovered that I was bearing some hurts which were unnecessary and extraneous. It was so good to offload them. The senior registrar, the psychologist, the nursing staff, all made themselves available. They spent hours listening, talking, just being there. I felt emotionally drained. But I was also drained of, and rid of, a great burden of hurt.

We all have our hurts. We are not all unable to walk, we are not all in pain, but we do all hurt. Some time ago I attended a Christian conference. After a meal, during coffee, I was sitting in the lounge talking with a Christian for whom I have the greatest respect. Around us were nearly a hundred other folk, chatting and drinking coffee. It was a very comfortable and contented atmosphere. We talked for a bit about me and my situation and then, looking around the room, he said, 'There is nobody here not hurting, nobody not bleeding.' They did not hurt outwardly, there was nothing to be seen. My hurt was obvious, crutches are hard not to notice. But some folk there may have had great hurts, broken hearts, damaged relationships, deep depressions, but they did not show. It did me good to be reminded that I was not alone in my hurt. It made me, for the remainder of that weekend, sit around more and listen to folk talking. We need to talk, we need to listen, we need to share, we need each other.

There is one who offers to help with our hurts, whose hands are outstretched to relieve us. To refuse his help is to commit ourselves to bearing our loads alone. Jesus said, 'Come to me, all you who are weary and burdened, and I will give you rest. Take my yoke upon you and learn from me, for I am gentle and humble in heart, and you will find rest for your souls. For my yoke is easy and my burden is light' (Matt. 11:28–30).

Insecurity.
Security is very much a topic of today, as is insecurity. We look at our children being brought up in Christian homes, which we would describe as secure, and favourably compare them to some of their schoolfriends from broken homes and insecure backgrounds. We think of security in terms of relationships, employment, and material possessions. We subconsciously define insecurity as the results of separation, divorce, redundancy and debt.

A dictionary defines security as, '(1). Untroubled by danger or apprehension; safe against attack, impregnable. (2). Reliable, certain not to fail or give way; in safe keeping, firmly fastened. (3). Having sure prospect of.' Many of us, much of the time experience, in terms of that definition, security. And it feels good.

In one moment of time, by the arrival of a letter, the ringing of a telephone, the knock at the door, or any of a large number of mundane possibilities, we can be robbed of our feelings of security. We can feel greatly troubled by danger and apprehension, unsafe against attack, vulnerable; unsure, uncertain of success or even stickability. In that moment we can feel out of control, foundationless, and with no certainties for the future.

Feelings of insecurity do not only come as a result of the dramatic. They can also arise because the mental picture we have of ourselves no longer fits the facts. Ill-health, disability and pain can blur that picture. When my pain became a continuing problem, I felt my security threatened.

I was no longer able to fill the role I saw as mine. I was a wife, a mother and a homemaker. I knew insecurity in all three areas. As a wife I felt diminished. As a mother I felt deflated. When the children came home from school I could not even return the spontaneity of a hug without first disentangling myself from my elbow crutches. As a homemaker? It is difficult to perch on crutches, hang out the washing, and retain equilibrium! I felt threatened. I experienced some of that dictionary definition, but only some of it. I knew the feeling of insecurity, but I did not know the fact of insecurity. Angus still loves me, the girls still hug me, and blow the washing!

Going back to our dictionary, I was troubled by pain, I was apprehensive about a future living with pain. I felt unsure how I would cope with pain. I did not know if I could. My feelings were in a knot. I recognised the experience as insecurity and that troubled me. I could not understand how, as a Christian, I could know insecurity. A comment in my Bible notes one day helped me a lot, it read, 'God gives security today, and glory tomorrow.' I wrote in my diary that morning,

'What an enormous relief to be certain that although I feel so insecure, I am in fact absolutely safe. My feelings and thoughts don't seem to co-ordinate just now.'

Security, I was reminded, is not only a feeling, it is also a fact. The teenager being thrust higher, and yet higher, in a rollercoaster knows that. She is secure, she knows she is secure, and so she hangs on tightly and enjoys the thrill of feeling insecure. When I thought it out that day, I realised that I was secure, I was certain of that. There was, however, no thrill in the feeling of insecurity, but I would hang on tightly to that security that only God can give.

Our definition contained four aspects of security which, for the Christian, are of paramount importance. 'Certain not to fail or give way.' Does this sound like the ultimate in conceit? We can learn some deep truths in the first chapter of Job. God knew the end from the beginning. He allowed Satan a leash long enough to test Job, to test him sorely, but not long enough to make him fail or give way. God knew Job's heart, God knew his faith, because he gave it to him. God gave him strength to withstand. But what of us, and what of now? God has made us a promise, 'God is faithful; he will not let you be tempted beyond what you can bear. But when you are tempted, he will also provide a way so that you can stand up under it' (1 Cor. 10:13). Notice, he does not promise a way of escape, but a way so that we can stand. Humanly speaking, we often fail, we often give way, but in terms of ultimate realities, our security is assured.

'In safe keeping, firmly fastened.'

Here again we have the fact of security. The Christian may lose her assurance, she may doubt her faith, but her assurance is not based on her feelings but on scriptural facts; nor is it based on the strength of her faith but on God's faithfulness. Jesus made a magnificent and mind-boggling statement about his people. I am sure that he understood that we would be incredulous about it, because he took care to repeat it for our benefit. Jesus said, 'I give them eternal life, and they shall never perish; no-one can snatch them out of my hand. My Father, who has given them to me, is greater than all; no-one can snatch them out of my Father's hand. I and the Father are one' (John 10:28–29).

'Having sure prospect of...'

In this world we have no sure prospect. We have no promise that our experience will be full of happiness, nor any threat that it will necessarily be full of grief. We share the lot of everyman. Our days will contain the various experiences which go to make up human life, A Christian does not live in some sort of sanctified cocoon. But the believer has a sure prospect. The believer has THE sure prospect. Jesus teaches us about the certainty of our prospect in the context of the uncertainties of life. He said, 'Do not let your hearts be troubled. Trust in God, trust also in me. In my Father's house are many rooms; if it were

not so, I would have told you. And I go to
prepare a place for you. And if I go and prepare a
place for you, I will come back and take you to
be with me that you may also be where I am'
(John 14:1–3).

Anger.

Even the word anger often produces in us
negative feelings. It reminds us of situations in
which we have been in receipt of someone's
anger, and other times when we have exhibited
our own. Christians, in the main, are uncomfortable with anger. Because of the negative circumstances with which we associate anger we
assume that anger itself is wrong.

We even apply this kind of reasoning to our
theological thinking. We stress that God is loving
and gracious and good and long-suffering. We
soft-pedal the fact that our God can be wrathful.
Not only are we uncomfortable with our own
anger, we are intensely embarrassed by God's.
But we must read and believe the totality of
God's Word. His Word is his self-revelation. Who
are we to pick and choose out of it what is to our
liking, and to forget conveniently what is not?

Where does this take us? We cannot deny the
anger of God, Scripture will not allow that. 'The
Lord's anger burned...' (Numb. 25:3); 'The Lord
became angry...' (1 Kings 11:9); 'We are con-
sumed by your anger and terrified by your
indignation' (Ps. 90:7). Nor can we say that the
anger of God is confined to the God of the Old
Testament. When we look at the life of God

Incarnate, we see anger. Jesus, the sinless Son of God, felt angry. Faced with inhumanity, Jesus, 'looked round at them in anger' (Mark 3:5). When the disciples turned the children away from Jesus, 'he was indignant' (Mark 10:14). Christ's overturning the tables of the money-changers in the temple area, is this not an angry response? (Matt. 21:12–13). Christ's rebuke of Peter, 'Get behind me, Satan,' does this not carry the force of anger? (Mark 8:33).

There is a conclusion we must draw from the anger of God. If to be angry is to sin, then God is a sinner like ourselves. If God is sinless, then anger can also be free from sin. This is verified for us in Scripture. 'In your anger do not sin' (Eph. 4:26). But immediately thereafter we have a warning that anger, which is not itself sinful, can so easily be twisted by Satan and become so. The passage reads, 'In your anger do not sin. Do not let the sun go down while you are still angry, and do not give the devil a foothold' (Eph. 2: 26–27).

God's anger is pure. It is directed against sin and the effects of sin. God's anger is not capricious, it is not unpredictable, it is not uncontrolled, and it does not continue for longer than is required.

If we translate this into human terms we must say four negative things about God's anger. Firstly, God's anger is not inappropriate. In Ezra 8:22 we see that it is directed against man's sinfulness. Secondly, God's anger is not temper. In Mark 3:5 we see it is related to Jesus' distress in response to inhumanity. Thirdly, God's anger is not the same as our smouldering vindictiveness. 'His anger lasts only for a moment, but his favour lasts for a lifetime' (Ps. 30:5). And fourthly, God's anger does not negate God's love. 'The Lord is compassionate and gracious, slow to anger, abounding in love' (Ps. 103:8).

Our main concern, however, is not with anger but with pain. Pain and suffering are among the direct consequences of the Fall. They mar God's creation, they detract from its perfection. Is it then inappropriate to react with anger? Pain may be a direct consequence of sin, as the drunken driver who is injured in an accident of his own making knows well. It may be a consequence of somebody else's sin, as the man knows who is knocked down in the same accident. Or an individual's pain may be part and parcel of the effects of the Fall on all mankind. But whatever is the cause of pain, whatever the source of suffering, it is still attributable to the Fall and to the consequent sinfulness of every human being. Is an angry reaction to sin, or to the results of sin, proper?

We accept the place of anger in broad terms. It has been responsible for vast sociological improvements. How else were little children stopped from climbing up chimneys in order to clean them? We see its place in the rearing and disciplining of our young folk. But when it comes to an angry reaction to our own circumstances, it becomes more of a problem to us. Surely we must conclude that it is not anger itself that is wrong, but what we do with it. Scripture gives us guidelines for the right and proper use of anger, indirectly and directly. Indirectly we study the anger of God and learn from that. But God's Word also has some very direct things to say on the subject.

When we react with anger there are some questions we must ask ourselves. Firstly, is my anger provoked by, and directed against, sin or sin's consequences, or is it caused by some hurt or offence which I have taken? Secondly, is the intensity of my anger commensurate with the provocation, or was the provoking factor just the 'last straw' and the wrath the result of a build-up of quite different things? Thirdly, is my anger of long standing? Is it still smouldering after days, or even weeks? Fourthly, is my anger unpredictable and capricious, or used carefully and, where appropriate, after due warning? Fifthly, is my anger in a situation really a result of my loving concern? In all these we can learn from Scripture by studying the anger of God.

The Bible also has some pertinent things to say to us on the subject quite directly. 'Refrain from anger and turn from wrath; do not fret — it leads only to evil' (Ps. 37:8). So anger has to be refrained from, rather than indulged in. Love 'is not easily angered, it keeps no record of wrongs' (1 Cor 13:5). The Christian should therefore work hard at not rushing into anger. And he is here specifically warned not to feed his anger by harbouring grudges. 'In your anger do not sin. Do not let the sun go down while you are still angry, and do not give the devil a foothold' (Eph. 4:26–27). Powerful teaching here — anger can indeed be righteous.

There is a place for anger, and an expression of anger, which is not wrong. Further, we are taught here that our anger must be of short duration. There is no place for smouldering wrath. But Scripture also recognises that even where anger is appropriate, even where it has a short life, we must take exceeding great care. When anything is lost, the owner ceases to have control over it. When a temper is lost, it is out of our control, and the devil, that great opportunist, is there, ready, and so willing to take it over for us. 'Do not give the devil a foothold.'

The person in pain can be affected by anger in two ways. By reacting with anger to his problem, and also by becoming short-tempered as a result of his pain. The Bible, as we have seen, addresses itself to him for his guidance in both these directions.

Like many Christians I have two problems with anger. I feel guilty even on those occasions where anger is expressed appropriately. And my anger is sometimes inappropriate. Pain sometimes shortens my fuse. Sleeplessness does the same. The result? Again, I feel guilty. Guilt and anger can become knotted together, and it is a work of patience to separate them.

In this area my conscience is quite unreliable. I have to look to the Bible to find whether or not my anger is righteous. When it is, my feelings of guilt must be disregarded. The Christian faith is founded on facts not feelings.

When my short fuse blows, God can even use that. I am sure that few things make as much of an impression on children as when their parents say that they are sorry. We impress on our little ones time and again, 'Say sorry.' Yet how rarely does a child have an apology from an adult? Anger has a place, but it has to be kept in it.

Confusion.

On one occasion, in hospital, I was asked how I felt. I replied that I felt confused. That night I did not sleep so I spent the waking hours working out what contributed to that feeling of confusion. I concluded that it was made up of some of the things we have been thinking about, and that at different times, all of them played a part in producing a degree of confusion.

I had clung to the verse, Romans 8:28, 'We know that in all things God works for the good of those who love him, who have been called according to his purpose.' I knew I loved the Lord. I believed with all my heart that he had called me to be his own. But I felt confused that all things did not seem to be working together for any good that I could see. I was helped enormously in this during a lecture in Systematic Theology when the subject was Suffering. The professor pointed out that we narrow that verse quite unscripturally. We think of 'our good' as being in terms of our comfort, our happiness, our success etc. But all things do work together for our ultimate good, and our ultimate good is that we are conformed to Christ and so prepared for heaven. That process, by necessity, will at times be hard, at times be painful, at times cause us great sorrow and suffering.

In terms of our eternal good may we share with John his vision of heaven — 'Then one of the elders asked me, "These in white robes — who are they, and where did they come from?". I answered, "Sir, you know". And he said, "These are they who have come out of great tribulation, they have washed their robes and made them white in the blood of the Lamb. Therefore, they are before the throne of God and serve him day and night in his temple ... For the Lamb at the centre of the throne will be their shepherd; he will lead them to springs of living water. And God will wipe away every tear from their eyes"' (Rev. 7:13—15,17).

Chapter 5

PAIN POSITIVE?

'Providence is not rolled upon unequal and
crooked wheels;
all things work together for the good of those
who love God,
and are called according to his purpose.
Ere it be long, we shall see the white side of
God's providence.'

Samuel Rutherford

We have thought about some of the difficulties
which can result from living with pain. To
maintain a balance, we must also consider the
benefits which that situation can produce. It is
perfectly obvious that pain has its own problems.
We do not have to look for them. It is also true
that even hard experiences have their blessed
side, but perhaps we do need to make an effort
to find it.

Let us think again about pain at its inception.
Pain, like suffering, illness, disease and death,
resulted from the fall of man. They are all part of
God's judgement on sinful mankind. We are
heirs of Adam's sin, and equally heirs to its
painful results. But we do not have a god who
delights in harsh judgement, a cruel and despotic
ruler who enjoys watching us squirm. The God
of the Bible is not such a god. Our God is just
and therefore judges. But he is a unity, and his
justice is not divorced from his love, nor his
righteousness from his mercy. So whatever our

painful experience is, whether it results from our own sin, someone else's sin, or is part of the lot of fallen mankind, even in that experience we shall, if we have eyes to see, find God graciously dealing with us.

Here we have three general causes of suffering which we must consider: personal sins, another's sins, humanity's sins. In each of them let us look for God-given blessings.

Pain as a result of personal sin.

All of us, day and daily, suffer the consequences of our own misdeeds. We are familiar with our own weaknesses and with what follows from them. In the longer term, some of us abuse our bodies, our minds, and our relationships, in such ways that very real pain is the outcome. What is the nature and purpose of this pain? Its nature is judgemental. If I live at a frenetic pace, at meetings every night, skipping meals to fit in yet more activities, the crashing headache which results the first time the pressure is off is a judgement on my lifestyle. If I overeat and under-exercise, any consequent problems are as much a judgement as if I had negligently run out in front of a bus and been knocked over by it. Some might argue that these are just instances of nature taking its course. But 'nature' is not an independent entity with a volition of its own, it is part of the created order. It follows that a 'natural' consequence is a God-determined consequence.

What is the purpose of the pain which is the

result of our own sin? If we think in terms of human relationships, there are occasions when a mother is constrained to punish her child in response to his wrongdoing, to make that child hurt, in order to do four things: to warn him of danger; to guide the child into safer circumstances; to teach him discipline in similar hazardous situations; and to make him remember the lesson he has learned. The judgement on the child's misdeed is painful, the consequent blessings are positive.

Pain, resulting from our own sin, can be a blessing because it can warn us of the danger of the situation we are in. Historically we see this in God's dealings with individuals. Jonah rebelled when God told him to go to Nineveh with a message to the people there from their Maker. He sailed off in the opposite direction with great haste. He certainly suffered for his rebellion during his incarceration inside the great fish. However, the result of that unpleasant and frightening episode was that, when he was released from his imprisonment, he praised God and set off for Nineveh. He learned, through his pain, the danger of his disobedience. As with Jonah, so with us. If we rebel against God's will and way we suffer his painful judgement, but we also receive the blessing of learning the danger of our foolishness.

Another blessing which can result from God's dealings with us due to our sinfulness is that of being set again in the right direction. We are like children who wander off the road into the gorse bushes. The path is marked, but we are easily distracted from our way. If it were not for the uncomfortable prickles from the bushes we might go on into the woods and lose our route altogether. Many a young person has had occasion to be grateful to his parents for keeping him on the Godward road, even when the discipline was painful and unappreciated at the time.

The pain which we suffer as a result of our own wrongdoing can teach us that in the future we must be more disciplined in a particular area of our lives. For example, some Christians live life at a hectic pace. They rush through each day as though it were their last, and as if God had somehow determined that a week's activity had to be crammed into it. As a result they may suffer the emotional pain of family breakdown, because they have not been in the home long enough to do any family build-up. They may have to endure the physical pain and distress due to exhaustion and burn-out. When we suffer judgement of that kind on our lifestyles we are well advised to question our priorities, and our use of time, and so enjoy the blessing of better ordered lives.

God's Word shows us the direction in which we should walk. In it he has revealed the 'Maker's instructions' for our personal and family lives, for our dealings with mankind in general, and indeed for our place in the whole order of creation. But we are chronically independent. We are sinful and rebellious. We choose, much of the time, to ignore Scripture's teaching and to turn our backs on godly guidance. We rush back to God and to our Bibles when things go wrong, when we hurt. Then when the sun comes out and the rain clouds vanish, we are tempted to lay aside God's Word until the next crisis. God speaks to us through Scripture, but many are the times when he uses pain, physical or emotional, to discipline us for our wrongdoing, and to remind us of our dependence on him for grace to overcome temptation.

Personal sinfulness can indeed result in personal pain, but it is our choice whether that pain is destructive and produces bitterness and hardness, or whether it is redeemed and used as a growth point for the future. What a God we have! He can see us in all our rebellion and need, and discipline us with a love that draws us back to himself. The Book of Hosea records God's dealings with his people who had wandered far from him. Near its conclusion we read, 'They will follow the Lord; he will roar like a lion. When he roars his children will come trembling from the west. They will come trembling like birds from Egypt, like doves from Assyria. I will settle them in their homes' (11:10—11). When we wander off in our sinful ways God may have to raise his voice to us, and shout to us through pain and suffering, to make us pay heed. But, when our attention is arrested, we will discover that what he is calling is that we are welcome to come back home, and to find a resting place in him.

PAIN POSITIVE?

Pain as the result of another's sin.

When we search our hearts and lifestyles for a cause of our pain, it may be perfectly clear that our suffering is not a result of any personal wrongdoing but is directly the consequence of somebody else's sin. We can think of numerous examples of this: the man struck down in a road accident caused by dangerous driving; the woman mugged on her way home from a visit; and the child assaulted by the school bully because he has a stammer.

How can any blessing come out of such a situation? Not easily. Scripture has some things to say to us when we are wronged, when we are sinned against. Firstly, the fact that someone hurts us is not a reason or excuse to act unworthily ourselves. The Psalmist prayed, 'Help me, for men persecute me without cause. They almost wiped me out from the earth, but I have not forsaken your precepts. Preserve my life according to your love, and I will obey the statutes of your mouth' (Ps. 119:86–88). The unjust suffering to which he was subjected turned him to God, and did not cause him to retaliate in such a way that would have 'forsaken God's precepts'.

Secondly, Jesus said, 'Love your enemies and pray for those who persecute you, that you may be sons of your Father in heaven' (Matt. 5:44). Jesus says that as we pray for our persecutors we will become more like sons and daughters of our Heavenly Father. What a wonderful truth – pain, even that pain which has been inflicted on us by the malice or negligence of another person, can help to conform us to the image of Christ.

Through our praying God will work a work of Grace and make us willing to forgive. We cannot truly pray and be unprepared to forgive. The two make a nonsense of each other. I am not saying that forgiveness is easy: it is not. To forgive someone who has been responsible for suffering, pain and distress is not a simple thing to do. Christ experienced that as he hung on the cross, suspended by the nails in his hands, listening to the crowds shouting to him to come down if he were able. Could it have been easy for him to pray to his Father to forgive the very folk who were causing his agony? So when we find it difficult to forgive we pray to one who understands. Our place is to be prepared to forgive. God will use our prayerfulness for the one who has wronged us to enable us to forgive should our forgiveness be sought. He does not demand of us what he is unwilling to produce within us.

Not only can God work this blessing in our own hearts, he can also use it to be of benefit to those who know us. Jesus said, 'Let your light shine before men, that they may see your good deeds and praise your Father in heaven' (Matt. 5:16). This does not mean that we live ostentatiously, our every altruistic act being done in public, but it is an instruction not to hide the light, the light of the gospel of Jesus Christ, not to hide it for shame or embarrassment, and not to keep from view the effects of God's enlightening of us. God can and will surely use the witness of the Christian who has been grievously wronged, who has suffered consequent pain and hurt, and who is not embittered but forgiving.

On a more universal scale, many millions of people suffer appalling pain and horrific distress because of man's inhumanity to man, and nation's brutality against nation. We only need to watch a television news bulletin for that truth to be imprinted on our minds. We, in the western world, use aerosols with abandon and a total disregard of the damage being done to the ozone layer, the consequences of which may be apparent in the lives of our children's children. And nationally, and internationally, we stockpile grain, build mountains of meat, create lakes of wine, and at the same time watch news clips showing us desperate poverty and dreadful hunger in Third World countries.

Some years ago we learned through the media of the plight of the people of Ethiopia. We had never before seen on our screens such horrendous reports. Nor have we in Britain ever responded to an appeal with such freedom. International inequality, man's inhumanity, and perhaps shame, caused us to react speedily and do what very little we could to alleviate the situation. Many folk carefully directed their money into agencies working in a preventive capacity. God used that terrible disaster, even that indescribable pain, to begin to break down the barriers of national boundaries, to cut through miles of red tape, in order to provide food when it was needed and to dig wells to help, in some little way, to prevent exactly the same thing happening again.

This is a small example in the face of the suffering which mankind endures, but an example all the same. We have a God who is able to turn disasters into opportunities. Our place is to recognise and make use of those opportunities.

Pain as the result of being part of fallen mankind.

God, we have seen, can overcome evil with good. He can turn pain to blessing, including the pain we bring on ourselves, and even the suffering which others inflict upon us. But what about the pain and suffering which is part of the bundle of being a fallen human being? Can he overrule for good the basic results of the fall? Can he use for blessing the processes of disease and decay and death which entered the world in Eden?

Peter, in his first letter, gives us some insight into how such suffering can be used to the glory of God and to our good. 'For a little while you may have had to suffer grief in all kinds of trials. These have come so that your faith — of greater worth than gold, which perishes even though refined by fire — may be proved genuine and may result in praise, glory and honour when Jesus Christ is revealed' (1 Pet. 1:7). In the Book of Job we see something of what Peter was meaning. Job, before the beginning of his sore trials, believed in God. 'This man was blameless and upright; he feared God and shunned evil' (1:1). After his first series of disasters, the bereft, homeless, believer was still able to praise God. 'The Lord gave and the Lord has taken away; may the name of the Lord be praised.' We stand back and humbly admire his faith. As Job's trials went on, not the least of them being the insensitivity of his companions, there is not a record of wavering faith in God but rather a revelation of deepening faith. When we listen to Handel's glorious music, do we remember that the words are an affirmation of even more glorious faith, wrung out of Job from the very pits of human degradation? 'I know that my Redeemer liveth, and that he shall stand at the latter day upon the earth: and though after my skin worms destroy this body, yet in my flesh shall I see God' (19:25–26). (AV)

We may well pray that we know nothing of Job's fearful testings, but such adverse circumstances as we do meet are purposed to refine our faith, to prove it genuine, and will result in praise and glory and honour when Jesus Christ is revealed. This is why James was able to say, 'Consider it pure joy, my brothers, whenever you face trials of many kinds, because you know that the testing of your faith develops perseverance' (James 1:2–3).

How is our faith refined through testing? In the verse from James we have one way. 'The testing of your faith develops perseverance.' This is again mentioned in Romans 5:3–5 where we have a list of potential positive gains out of our loss of ease. 'We rejoice in the hope of the glory of God. Not only so, but we also rejoice in our sufferings, because we know that suffering produces perseverance; perseverance, character; and character, hope. And hope does not disappoint us, because God has poured out his love into our hearts by the Holy Spirit, whom he has given us.' Suffering must not embitter the Christian, but should rather bear the fruits of perseverance, character and hope.

Perseverance.
To persevere is to pursue a steadfast purpose, to maintain sight of an aim and to persist towards its realisation. Suffering and pain can indeed encourage perseverance both practically and spiritually. Pain concentrates the mind, and demands that the sufferer work out his priorities and devote what energy and enthusiasm he has to a limited number of aims. This can be a great blessing, because it can enable him to clear out much of the clutter of activity and the muddle of thought which has accumulated over the years. It can enable him to rethink his use of time and talents. 'Let us throw off everything that hinders and the sin that so easily entangles, and let us run with perseverance the race marked out for us' (Heb. 12:1).

In the following verse we have our aim. 'Let us fix our eyes on Jesus, the author and perfecter of our faith, who for the joy set before him endured the cross, scorning its shame, and sat down at the right hand of the throne of God.' Jesus endured the cross for the joy set before him, the joy of presenting his redeemed people to his Father in heaven. May we endure our suffering, persevering for the joy set before us, the joy of being like Jesus, of being presented to the Father by the Son, of spending eternity in his glorious presence.

Character.
Our character is what differentiates us from everyone else, what makes us distinctive and unique. It is not our physical attributes but our personal qualities. It is not our height but our depth, not our colouring but the tone of our lives. It is not what someone sees when they meet us, but what they feel after they have left us.

God can use suffering to develop our characters. The woman who remembers her pain and heartache when she had a miscarriage is not the same woman who tells someone else in that position that she should forget it and become pregnant again right away. Her suffering has made her different, she remembers her experience, and puts her arm round her friend and cries with her.

Only the person who has gone through the despair of depression has the character and insight to speak right to the heart of the sad soul who is depressed. When I was down, after the trauma of drug withdrawal, a Christian friend spoke to me. He knew depression and said, 'I know where you are because I have been there myself. I recognise the countryside. One day you will be grateful for having been there, because you will be able to help someone else in the same situation. But I wish to God neither of us had had to go through it.' He had the right to say that, because his suffering had changed his character and given him that right.

Only those who have suffered know, in any real sense, what the sufferer is going through. Only those who have known pain to the point of distraction can have a real understanding of the poor soul who is brain-blown. Others can help, of course they can. That is one of the gifts of God's common grace. But some, not gifted in that respect, have their characters changed into the shape of their own experience of suffering. They are therefore able, by the grace of God, to stand with others in their time of need and be the kind of people who can help.

We would not choose to suffer, we would not opt for pain or distress. But given suffering, pain and distress, let us make a determined choice to grow from them rather than to be diminished by them.

Hope.

Anyone who is going through a difficult time, hopes it will pass, and for most folk it does. Is that what is meant by perseverance producing hope? Surely there is more to it than that. If we think of that great chapter on the subject of love, 1 Corinthians 13, we remember that there we have twelve verses describing Christian love, then in the last verse, two other Christian graces are mentioned. 'Now these three, faith, hope and love. But the greatest of these is love.'

We have discussed perseverance as a result of suffering, but perseverance of what? Surely of faith. We have thought about character, but character characterised by what? Surely by love. Here we come to the third of the three great things we are recommended to pursue, Christian hope. When the believer is suffering, when his pain is pressing, when his spirit is heavy, when his faith is weak, there is the place for Christian hope. 'Why are you cast down, O my soul? Why so disturbed within me? Put your hope in God, for I will yet praise him, my Saviour and my God' (Ps. 42:5).

The psalmist's hope was that he should YET praise God. He was finding it so hard to praise him, yet he did, and he believed he would continue to do so in the future. But the believer not only has a hope for praising God in this world, he has an eternal hope. Even should his suffering continue to the end of his life on earth, YET he will praise God.

The Christian's eternal hope is nothing vague and nebulous. 'Faith is being sure of what we hope for and certain of what we do not see' (Heb. 11:1). The faith of the believer is based on the certainty of his hope. And his hope is based on the promises of the eternal Son of the eternal God, who does not lie. Jesus said, 'I go and prepare a place for you, I will come back and take you to be with me' (John 14:3).

How does the sure hope of the Christian relate to his pain? The friend of Jesus knows with assurance that although his pain may last until the moment he dies, it will ONLY last until then. Suffering is limited to this world and to the time we spend in it. Heaven would not be heaven if we had to suffer there. When we die we will leave behind all sin, and all the consequences of sin, all sorrow, all suffering, and every pain. There are no diseases in heaven, nothing will decay there. 'God will wipe away every tear from their eyes', and no more will be shed.

Many weary Christians know what it is to hope for heaven, to desire to cast off their painful bodies and put on eternal white robes. Paul records this as being his experience. 'Now we know that if the earthly tent we live in is destroyed, we have a building from God, an eternal house in heaven not built with human hands. Meanwhile we groan, longing to be clothed with our heavenly dwelling.... We are confident, I say, and would prefer to be away from the body and at home with the Lord'(2 Cor. 5:1,2,8).

I know the longing to which Paul refers. There have been times when my greatest consolation has been that my pain is but for my lifetime, and that is just a moment in the context of eternity. I have, however, seen much of God's goodness over the time I have suffered. Pain has been used in ways for which I am profoundly grateful.

Earlier we noticed that pain concentrates the

mind. It throws things into sharp relief. I have certainly found this to be the case. It has made me realise afresh the preciousness of relationships, because there have been times I have had to rely on them so much and I have found them to be strong and true.

It has opened the door to meeting new people and to making new friends, and these are folk I have met with no pretence. I did not get to know them when I had on my Sunday clothes or my 'I'm coping' face. I met them in wards and clinics and surgeries where we all felt a little vulnerable and, consequently, where we shared a little more deeply.

I got to know Agnes. She and I were in the same hospital ward. We could not spend much time together as she had recently had a leg amputated and, because of complications, was on bed rest. I was confined by the restrictions imposed by having a drip attached to my arm. But the ways of patients are wonderful, and we did manage to find the means of getting together on occasions! Before Agnes died a few weeks later, she had found faith in Jesus. What had impressed her, and made her think, was the time she had spent watching my visitors with me. I was blessed by having lots of friends, mostly Christian friends, come to see me. They so obviously cared, they read to me, and they prayed with me. Agnes said that she had known about Jesus all of her life but she had never before met folk who knew him personally. She had recognised in the friends who visited me people who knew and loved Jesus. Two weeks after I was discharged Agnes lost her other leg, and a little while later she lost her life. I visited her a day or two before she died. As I got up to leave she asked me to pray with her, as my friends had prayed with me. When I left there were tears in her eyes, but not of self-pity. We both knew that we would not meet again this side of eternity, but that in heaven we would.

The friendship I had with Agnes was one of the deep blessings which would not have come about but for God's provident use of my pain. Another rich experience happened some fifteen months later. At an evening service our minister preached from Isaiah 43, God's words in verses 1 to 3. 'Fear not, for I have redeemed you; I have summoned you by name; you are mine. When you pass through the waters, I will be with you; when you pass through the rivers, they will not sweep over you. When you walk through the fire you will not be burned; the flames will not set you ablaze. For I am the Lord, your God, the Holy One of Israel, your Saviour.' During that service I was overwhelmed by the realisation that I was grateful, deeply grateful, for the experience of passing through the waters and so knowing the intimate closeness of Almighty God. I would not have chosen to have gone that way. I would not choose to repeat it. But I am so, so thankful for it.

How reassuring it is to know that God can use even our pain and suffering, even our disease and decay, to work good in our hearts and in the hearts of others. We have a wonderful God. Let us now give some thought to what he can do with the last enemy — death.

Death is the result of sin. It is the wage paid for claiming independence from God. 'The wages of sin is death' (Rom. 6:23). Disease and decay are the instalments by which we pay the price. We are none of us exempt. The price which is owed to Almighty God must be paid. This is a hard truth, and a Bible truth, but it is not the whole truth. 'The wages of sin is death, but the gift of God is eternal life in Jesus Christ our Lord.' (Rom. 6:23). How can this be?

We share the curse of mankind since the sin of Adam and Eve, and like them we are banished from fellowship with God. The cherubim and flaming sword which prevented our first parents from returning to Eden symbolise man's total inability to return to God. There was a great gulf and barrier between man and God that man could do nothing to span. The nature of his heart was inclined towards evil and away from good, and from God.

Man could not bridge the chasm, but God could, and God did. He spanned it with a cross. He made a way for man to come to him, because he first came to man. God was constrained by his own love to reach out, at inestimable cost, to lost mankind. 'God so loved the world that he gave his one and only Son, that whoever believes in him shall not perish but have eternal life' (John 3:16). The price we owe is death, the gift he gives is life.

Christ became man and lived and died as all men do. But his life was radically different from the life of even the best of men. He was sinless, perfect, faultless. He was the first man since Adam who did not transgress God's law and who therefore did not have to pay the price of sin. He so lived that he did not need to die. His perfection is attested in Scripture and history. Yet, in all time, no death has been so well documented as the crucifixion of Jesus Christ, the Son of God. Here we have a great mystery. The wages of sin is death, but the one death in the whole world, and for all time, about which we have the most evidence, is the death of the sinless Jesus, the only one from whom the price did not need to be exacted.

Why did Christ die? He did not die to pay the price of his own sins, he died on account of ours. Jesus 'was delivered over to death for our sins and was raised to life for our justification' (Rom. 4:25). What a glorious gospel we have in this verse. Christ paid the price sinners owed to God. God accepted that payment and verified his acceptance by raising Jesus from the dead.

Does that mean that we are living in a new age, an age in which we are free from the debt consequent upon our sinfulness? If we have faith in Jesus, incredibly, this is the case! 'Righteousness from God comes through faith in Jesus Christ to all who believe' (Rom. 3:23). Does this mean that God's anger no longer burns against those who believe? This is exactly the truth! 'We have now been justified by his blood, how much more shall we be saved from God's wrath through him! For if, when we were God's enemies, we were reconciled to him through the death of his Son, how much more, having been reconciled, shall we be saved through his life! Not only is this so, but we also rejoice in God through our Lord Jesus Christ, through whom we have received this reconciliation' (Rom.5:9–11).

Do we realise the implications and the glory of what we are thinking? God made man perfect. Man chose of his own free will to 'do his own thing'. He sinned. He therefore owed God the price his sin cost. He owed God his life. God, in his love, sent his own Son, perfect and sinless, to become the ransom price, in order that we might have eternal life. The catch? There is no catch. This new life in Christ is available to all who recognise their sinful state and believe in him. 'If we confess our sins, he is faithful and just and will forgive us our sins and purify us from all unrighteousness' (1 John 1:9). The gospel offer is made in Scripture to all, and none who come to Christ in faith will not find eternal life in him. Jesus said, 'My Father's will is that everyone who looks to the Son and believes in him shall have eternal life, and I will raise him up at the last day' (John 6:40).

Can we take in what a great God we have? The cruel cross on which Jesus died, he turned into a bridge between God and man. The death which Christ endured, God has accepted as the substitute for that of all believers so that they should have eternal life. God took the most calamitous moment in the history of the cosmos and made it the most glorious point of all eternity!

We all suffer death as the result of Adam, let us look with John at his vision of heaven as a result of the death and resurrection of Christ. 'I looked and there before me was a great multitude that no-one could count, from every nation, tribe, people and language, standing before the throne and in front of the Lamb. They were wearing white robes and were holding palm branches in their hands. And they cried out in a loud voice: 'Salvation belongs to our God, who sits on the throne, and to the Lamb.' All the angels were standing round the throne .... they fell down on their faces before the throne and worshipped God, saying: 'Amen! Praise and glory and wisdom and thanks and honour and power and strength to our God for ever and ever. Amen!'

For the Christian, then, death is the gateway to heaven, the entrance to the throne-room of Almighty God. Paul said, 'For to me, to live is Christ and to die is gain... I am torn between the two: I desire to depart and be with Christ, which is better by far...' (Phil. 1:21–23). The sting of death was sin, but Christ became sin for his people, and so removed the sting from the death of the believer. Paul rejoices in this, 'Death has been swallowed up in victory. Where, O death, is your victory? Where, O death, is your sting? ... Thanks be to God! He gives us the victory through our Lord Jesus Christ' (1 Cor. 15: 54–57).

Chapter 6

MY COMPANIONS

'I hold out my pain to you.
You taught me how to smooth
Its jagged edge
With calmness,
Restoring to me
Some of the person-ness
Pain dulled.

I hold out my hurt to you.
Help me to untie
That tangled knot
Of bindweed.
With gentleness
Unloose its tendrils
From my life.

I trust my tears to you,
Precious jewel drops
Of shed emotion,
Longing for release
To be set free.
Walk with me
Through the hurts
That feed the well-spring.
Walk with me,
I trust you with my tears.'

For all of us, whatever our circumstances, relationships are important. We are social creatures, we were not made to be alone. When

God created Adam, he said, 'It is not good for the man to be alone' (Gen. 2:18). From the earliest point of the history of mankind it has been recognised that man was made for fellowship. A man is incomplete without relationships. This is one of the respects in which we bear the image of God. God is a unity, but he is a unity of three persons who eternally share fellowship with one another.

The first relationship which the earliest man enjoyed was with the God who created him. God then made for him a helper, a woman. Here we have Adam's second relationship, the God-given, and divinely appointed relationship of a man with a woman. Later came the parent/child connection, the sibling relationship, then cousins, aunts, and uncles, until society gained its structure. From our first parents until today God has ordained that man should not be alone. From his birth he is surrounded by parents, family, extended family, society and national and international frameworks beyond his ken. The whole business of growing up is that of finding where we fit into the complex structures which make up our society. The child who grows up without the rigidity of structured relationships can have very real problems working out who he really is.

As the years pass we can become very comfortable in our relationships, not necessarily in a rut, but content and accepting the secure feelings which result from a deep friendship or a happy marriage. We know how things tick in the relationship. We know the role we play in it. We are aware of the contribution we make to it, and we accept the benefits we gain from it. Then suddenly, or perhaps not so suddenly, there is a change in the accepted arrangement, one person cannot play her former role, yet now more than ever needs all the benefits. One of the parties may become ill, suffer redundancy, may have an accident, or require surgery. There results a threat, not to the relationship per se, but to what the relationship is perceived to be. The relationship remains the same, but the roles within it have to be rearranged. What is true of the person to person relationships of friendship and marriage is also true within the larger structures of society.

When Angus and I first knew each other I could walk for miles. We spent our 'getting to know each other' time walking along Scottish shores and country lanes, not to mention remote churchyards as we pursued our interest in genealogy! I had some discomfort when I walked but, as I had experienced that all of my life, I had learned to live with it. In any case, getting to know Angus made it worth putting up with a sore ankle.

By 1980, after pushing our three daughters in prams and push-chairs for five years, I discovered that I could not really walk very well unless I had something to lean on. When riding in a push-chair was below the dignity of Alison, our youngest, I had a problem — one cannot go around pushing an empty pram! At that point I was equipped with a caliper and was again able to walk for miles, if a little more slowly, and with a squeak!

Now, after nineteen years of marriage, and with three growing up girls, I am more handicapped. My problem is pain. My mobility is severely affected by it. I can walk using crutches, but not far, and not fast. I have, from time to time, the problems attendant on pain, the difficulties discussed in earlier chapters.

As each one of these stages has been reached it has been necessary to rethink the relationships of which I am a part, and to redefine the role which I see to be mine. Because my condition has been of long duration, and the steps down to my present reduced level of mobility have sometimes been years apart, I have had time to become comfortable and secure in my relationships at each stage. I am grateful for that. This has had two results. Firstly, each time I have had to see my role anew it has seemed to diminish yet again. Secondly, I can remember that it has worked out before and I can be sure that the same will happen on this occasion.

Over the years it has been so reassuring that, although Angus has had to watch me lose my mobility, he has never made me feel that these changes have altered our relationship. I choose my words carefully, circumstances have changed our relationship, but he has never made me feel that was the case, at least not in any negative sense.

No relationship is static, least of all a marriage.

MY COMPANIONS

In 1985, just a year before my problem came to a head, we had moved from a small country town to the city so that Angus could train for the Christian ministry. That changed our relationship. I was no longer married to a man reaching middle age, and well up in his profession. I was married to a student who spent the days at college and the evenings at his desk with his books. Prior to that he had, for the most part, left his work in the office and spent the evenings with the family. We had discussed, before making that move, the changes that would result. One of them was that he would spend a time in the early evenings with the girls, then I would take over whatever the activity was, and he would return to his studying. That move of course changed our relationship.

Another difference was the degree of my involvement with Angus's work. Prior to moving he did his work in the office. My only role in that was to let him offload the pressures at the end of the day, and appreciate the often very entertaining stories he brought home with him from working life. That certainly changed. During his first year in college I found myself revising my rather elderly knowledge of Greek, and discussing the finer points of Hebrew grammar. I tried to keep abreast of the subjects he was studying, at least in general terms, enjoying the stimulation of discussing them late into the evenings. That was an enormously companionable time. It was to stand us in good stead for the traumatic years which were to follow.

PAIN, MY COMPANION

The nerve in my ankle was severed at the beginning of Angus' second year and my mobility was much reduced. That year was very different from the previous one. I no longer found the days long enough and my energy sufficient to run the home and family, type Angus's essays, and read widely and deeply. I struggled to keep going at all. I was in a wheelchair and in a lot of pain. Suddenly my situation changed from being one of contributing to family life, and of helping and supporting my husband in his studies, to feeling that I was a cause of concern and of extra work to everyone in the home, and not much good to anyone. My self-esteem plummeted.

Angus had to devote much more time to home and family. I had little energy to go over even the shortest Greek vocabulary. My mother came regularly and helped a lot. A home-help was of enormous value in reducing the dust level. And the girls then aged 11, 10 and 8 were marvellous. But the more folk needed to do for me, the more redundant I felt. I was so used to being the one who helped the others. I found it difficult to be on the receiving end.

Particularly hard for me was knowing that I was not helping Angus with his studies. To make up for the extra time he had to spend doing other things he got up in the early hours of the morning and did not pack up his books until it was morning again. Over that time my medication was such that I slept. I was asleep when he got up and I was asleep when he went to bed.

MY COMPANIONS

The hour when we sat down together after dinner to watch the news – I slept then too. That year we reaped the benefit of the depth of our relationship. We drew out some of what we had invested over the years. We were living on the interest.

In the late summer of 1987, before the beginning of Angus's final year, it was realised that I had become addicted to Methadone. This had been prescribed to reduce pain which was at a level that had been threatening to drive me out of my mind. It was necessary for a time in order to restore me to being a person. I had become some kind of pain-endurance machine. The dosage was reduced slowly and carefully, but the result of stopping it finally was devastating. For days I felt worms crawling all over me. I saw strange animals everywhere. I jerked and writhed and my head seemed to burst. I longed to be held close, and I could not bear to be touched. Pain had threatened my mind: drug withdrawal blew it.

For the first time in my relationship with him I was totally dependent on Angus. He sat on the bed and quietly read psalms to me. He did not even know if I could hear him. But for me the only two certainties I had during those indescribable days were, that Angus loved me, and that God was even nearer to me than Angus sitting there on the edge of the bed.

A cousin once described me as the family's 'earth mother'; for a couple of weeks after that experience I was treated like the family's antique china. I had always been aware of being in the supportive role of wife and mother. I had to learn the humble role of being supported, being cared for and cossetted, not only by Angus and my mother, but by three wee girls and some dear friends. In any other circumstances I would have found that difficult. But after the trauma I had been through, it was as comforting to my bruised mind as a warm bath is to a weary body.

Angus's final year at College was as different from the first two as they had been from each other. With help from surgery, from my doctor and from a specialist in pain relief, I was able to assume again a more normal role. The girls, who were that bit older, helped more in the house. I had a splendid home-help who did, not what she thought needed done, but what I could not do.

The previous year I had been living on the benefits of intellectual and sometimes spiritual input from the past. That year I joined Angus at College and sat in on the Systematic Theology lectures. Attending the classes four mornings each week contributed to restoring to me the balance I so much needed. The year had its ups and downs. I was in hospital for a number of weeks during it. Pain was still a real problem. But the regular and systematic study of the great doctrines of God's Word helped me to regain my equilibrium. I identified with the psalmist who said, 'If your law had not been my delight, I would have perished in my affliction' (Ps. 119:92). The mental activity required by the course was stimulating. And being part of the community of a small college was enormously refreshing. Three weeks spent in our local rehabilitation hospital at the end of that year helped consolidate the gains, and enabled me to work out some of my muddle-mindedness. By the time summer came, and Angus qualified, I felt I had recovered personhood and was able to function again as a more responsive wife and involved mother.

Anyone reading the account of the three years we spent as a student family will see it as being a negative and dreadfully difficult time. It was indeed very hard. But strangely, at the end of it, we both agree that in some ways it has been the best years of our life together. That sounds quite absurd, but I think the basis of that blessing is two-fold. God has been closer to us than our problems, and in his infinite providence he has used the hard times to throw our relationship into sharp focus. What we perhaps took for granted before, we now count a gift of inestimable value.

Our marriage is not the only relationship which has been affected by the change in my condition. Isabel, Ruth and Alison have also been intimately involved. In the space of just over a year they moved to a new part of the country, another school, an unfamiliar congregation and away from all their friends. Angus stopped having free evenings to spend with them and was most often surrounded by weighty tomes in strange languages. I became crippled, for a time virtually housebound, and unable to do much of what had been accepted as normal. They were required to do more to help than they had before, and certainly more than their friends did. The little world in which they lived was turned on its head.

There was also, for the older two girls, a sense of déjà vu. Years before, when their sister was too small to remember, their uncle died. Adam was a partner in a firm of solicitors in Elgin, where Angus was librarian. He was very much part of our little family. He had a leg amputated in order to prevent the spread of cancer which had been discovered in his foot. Over the following eighteen months he had chemotherapy, and after each treatment he lived with us until he was well enough to look after himself again. He was a Christian and endured his illness with great courage and dignity. Eventually his treatment was ended. Just a few weeks later he slipped into a coma and died, aged 31.

Seven years passed, then the girls were to find their mum having real problems with her ankle, and on occasions sharing a hospital ward with patients who were amputees. This was very hard for them. Seeds of concern and doubt sprang up in their minds. It was especially difficult because they had problems expressing what was in their hearts. It was not easy for us either. If we brought up the subject of their uncle we felt we were confirming them in their anxieties.

In order to allay their fears we kept them very well informed about what was happening. They knew more about my condition than I would have chosen that children of their ages should. But circumstances determined that to be necessary. It was better that they were intelligently aware of the reason for my pain and what was being done for it, than that they should eat their hearts out with worry.

It is never easy for the children in a family when one of the parents is ill or incapacitated and regularly an in-patient in hospital. It poses a real threat to them, even when Gran is imported to keep the home running as near normally as possible. Every child is different, and our three girls reacted to the situation according to their distinct natures. One covered her concern by being a bit blasé and off-hand, another could not hide her feelings and was often quite upset, and the third was very matter-of-fact and practical. Each had to be met at the level of her own need. And they all had to take care not to irritate each other by their idiosyncratic responses to the situation.

On occasions I have been aware that instead of the mother mothering her children the children were mothering their mother. This is not appropriate. Families in our situation have somehow to work out how to maintain right relationships even when, in practical terms, the roles are altered.

Over the years the girls have had to assume more responsibility for housework: consequently we have had to work out a way in which I can still be their mother and running the home while they in fact do quite a bit of the work. We

tried variously to do this, and our success fluc-
tuated. As they got older their friends started
taking paper rounds and finding other ways of
earning money. We suggested then that they do
a specific set of chores each week and that we
pay them, when they reach the paper-round age,
the same wage as their friends get for doing their
jobs. Until that age, their chores are less and their
pay is too. Having said this we do not, and
would not, overload them with work. They
probably have a friend or two who does as much
because both parents work. But what we are
doing is, not so much paying to get work done,
but having the necessities done in such a way
that the relationships are kept on an appropriate
footing. We did not appreciate one friend who
asked the girls when they were unwell if they got
sick pay!

Had we drawn the blueprint for life in our
home and family, the plan would have been
different. Dad and Mum would have been fit and
able, the girls would have glowed with good
health, and the rest would have read like a story
book. But, in the providence of God, that was
not to be. Instead, we have had real problems,
and continuing problems, but God has even
used them to the blessing of our children.

Isabel, Ruth and Alison have become more
aware of the needs of others. They know that
inside a handicapped body there lives a normal
person. A long-term friendship with Lynda, who
has Down's Syndrome, had already shown them
that personality is not the prerogative of only the

intellectually clever. Whatever the girls do with their lives, their experiences of having had a disabled parent will allow them to do it with more care, deeper concern and less of the prejudice which results from thinking that a person is only what can be seen from the outside.

Relationships beyond the immediate family widen like ripples in a pool. We have had much cause to be grateful for our extended family. Both grannies have helped enormously, practically, financially, and by being such supportive people. My mother has taken over the reins of the household when I was not able. Angus's mother has given us the money to pay our home help to do the rest. There have been occasions when I have found it irksome to be in a dependent relationship with my mother. Having been out of the family nest for a decade and a half perhaps that is not surprising. Once or twice I have responded with childish irritability when I have felt that the running of our home was being taken out of my control. There is a fine line along which carer and cared-for must travel, so that both the relationship and dignity remain intact.

When we extend the ripples yet wider we find family members who love and show it. What a blessing the telephone is to a family scattered across the countryside. What a difference our situation must make to the annual profits of British Telecom! The knowledge of being part of a larger unit, of being in the hearts and minds and prayers of folk dear to us is very humbling, and so reassuring.

PAIN, MY COMPANION

Within our family we have many dear friends. We also have friends who feel very much part of the family. We moved nearly 200 miles to Edinburgh just a year before I became disabled by pain. Consequently, with only a few exceptions, the friends we saw most often we had known only for that length of time. We could have felt very much on our own. But God knew our needs before making us aware of them. He also supplied them most graciously.

Within our close neighbours he provided dear Christian folk, with some of whom we were enjoying fellowship within days of our arrival in the city. Two couples locally were especially practical in their caring. Robert and Lorraine knew ill-health and disability in their own family and, recognising our areas of need and concern, did their best to answer them. Colin and Rosemary provided a warm welcome and coffee one evening every two or three weeks, and the opportunity to relax and enjoy the warmth of Christian fellowship with them.

Because mobility has been a real problem, I have been so grateful to friends who have transported me to and fro in their cars. We had known Sheana and her sister Sandra for a number of years before we moved, having met annually at a Christian conference. Sheana retired prior to our arrival in the city – or perhaps it was because of our impending arrival! I certainly would have found difficulty getting about but for her willingness to put her car at my disposal. She has read many books and knitted up dozens of balls of wool in hospital out-patient departments over the last four years.

These and other friends have had something very important in common. They have been able to help without allowing our relationships to become lop-sided. There has been nothing of condescension in their approach. I appreciated so much those occasions when Rosemary came along with some problematic sewing, when Lorraine felt able to offload her concerns, and when Sheana made it clear that she too needed shopping, that our joint visits to the supermarket were not only for my benefit.

We have, each one of us, an ever-widening circle of acquaintances. Our pivotal point is within our families. Outside of that we have the friendships of the folk to whom we choose to be close. For the Christian there are also those friends who are within the congregation to which he belongs, and in the wider church. A humanist friend once told me that she envied the Christian only one thing – the fact that wherever he goes he has a ready-made support structure in his local church. I would not have put it quite like that but, for us, it has certainly proved to be true!

When we went to live in the city so that Angus could begin his studies for the ministry, we moved from a small congregation of some thirty folk, to Buccleuch and Greyfriars Free Church where there seemed to be more meetings held some weeks than there were evenings to hold them in. Tea and coffee was served in the hall after the morning service. On our first Sunday there, our youngest daughter, who was just seven, said that she did not know how she would get to know all the people, there were just too many legs! That child's eye view said it all.

Our reception from the folk belonging to the legs was warm and welcoming! The members of that congregation take to their hearts the students and student families who arrive year by year from different parts of the country and far-flung corners of the world. During our time in Edinburgh there were more Korean little ones in the crêche than Scots! We were aware, from the beginning of our membership, of the care and concern of the congregation for us. We knew of their prayerfulness on our behalf, especially during two periods in our first year when one of the girls was unwell and needed to be in hospital.

From the beginning of our second year, when my problem became acute, the congregation upheld us most movingly. Over my times in hospital I was visited regularly. Car drivers gave lifts to the family so they could visit me. Cards and letters have came with the most thoughtful of messages. When I was at home transport was arranged so that I could attend church easily. People were not shy to show the concern they felt.

Not only were we been blessed by the caring nature of our minister and congregation, we were also very aware of their prayers on our behalf. I was conscious that, each Sunday as I went down the aisle to the chair which had been thoughtfully provided for me, folk were reminded of my need for prayer. My handicap was obvious. My crutches were on the floor beside my chair. The carefulness and prayerfulness, which was the congregational response, was almost tangible.

For some months I had a struggle with my feelings regarding the congregation. I knew of their concern and I was assured of their prayers. That was all positive. My response, however, was sometimes negative. As I went into church, so far as anyone could see, my condition was no better. Some Sundays I made my way along the aisle feeling like a disappointment. I saw myself as an unanswered prayer. This disconcerted me and made me think. Then I remembered my brother-in-law. Adam had lost his fight against cancer, despite great prayerfulness on his behalf. But those of us who knew him were aware that prayer was being answered, not in terms of the healing of his body, but in the preparation of his soul for heaven, and in the gifts of grace and dignity which were his until the end of his life on earth. What I had seen as answered prayer in relation to him, I hope others see in me.

One of the blessings which I mentioned regarding our marriage has also been true of our friendships. It is so easy to take for granted what you always have. Throughout our lives we have had good friends. We have enjoyed rich fellowship. These relationships have been especially tried and tested over the last few years and they have not been found wanting. We knew we were cared for in Elgin. We had been there fourteen years and had time to love and be loved, especially in our church. What we discovered was that deep wells can be sunk into friendship within a much shorter time, and that the God who knew what our needs were going to be, in that and in every other respect, went before us and supplied them in abundance.

Our friends from Morayshire did not forget us either. Miles are no bar on care, nor are they a limitation on prayer. I went back for a week-end during what was a particularly difficult time for me, and came home refreshed and deeply moved by the experience.

Most of us have a wide circle of acquaintances, family and friends near and far. But there are other folk we meet day by day, the folk with whom we work, and those who meet us as a consequence of their job. Among those whom I have come to know over the last few years have been an interesting selection of doctors, nurses and others in the medical field. Although these are relationships which are of a professional rather than a personal capacity, they are nonetheless of enormous importance.

I was once asked if I was employed. Because of the number of out-patient appointments which I had attended in the recent past, I was tempted to say that I worked part-time for the local health board! Most of us, for much of the time, visit our family doctor occasionally, rarely see a hospital specialist, and can spend years without being an in-patient. Others have a different experience. They take a book to read in the hospital waiting-room because they know the magazines there by heart!

When we put ourselves into the care of a general practitioner, a hospital doctor, or any other medical professional, we enter into a relationship in which we invest a great deal. Jointly, with them, we share the care of our bodies and of our minds. On sending our children to school we take great interest in the teachers who look after them and are responsible for their education. We see them as people, and we accept the appropriateness of trust, and the need of good relationships, in that context. We would strenuously deny that we see our children as empty heads to be filled with facts by characterless machines called teachers. At the same time we sometimes act as though we see our ill bodies and upset minds as mechanical devices which have gone wrong, which with the help of cool, efficient and anonymous engineer/ doctors can be put right again. If this is our way of thinking we deny ourselves therapeutic relationships, and our doctors job-satisfaction.

I know doctors are human, after all some of them are cousins, uncles, aunts and friends of our family! No kind of metamorphosis takes place when an M.B., Ch.B. is conferred. The man in the white coat is still a man. For so long have we treated our medical folk as one step from divine, some of them need a little nudge in the direction of remembering that the patient in the pyjamas is still a person! The relationship must be two-way to be of real benefit.

Our primary medical care is carried out by our family doctors, and how we relate to them is of vast importance. When we moved home we took great care over the selection of a family doctor. We did not just go to the local surgery on the corner. We specifically took advice in order to find one who would best appreciate Alison's problems. Little did we then know that he was also the right person to hold me together during what were going to be traumatic years. Of that we were ignorant, but God was not.

Soon after we arrived, we took the children and introduced ourselves to Dr. Murray. It did not seem to be a good idea to take one of the girls to meet him first as a stranger when she was ill, and to expect them to relate well to each other in those circumstances. We were impressed. The girls are very different and he treated them as individuals. He did understand Alison's difficulties. He had chocolate beans which he produced for children visiting him. In a certain drawer she knew that there was a packet of different sweets which were allowed in her diet. They were not only for her, he occasionally ate them too!

There is a two-way caring in a doctor/patient relationship. We do not expect our family doctor to look after our health without our being concerned for him. He diagnoses our problems and treats us. We pray for him. He visits us when we are ill. We send him a card when he is. We do not rush in to his surgery and pour out our aches and pains without the courtesy of asking after his health. He does not write a prescription without looking up at us.

Can I be specific in my appreciation of our family doctor and, in so doing, demonstrate some of the points which I have found to be of prime importance. Over the time we were Dr. Murray's patients, I saw him often. He was always close enough to be approachable, but distant enough to be objective. In the situations in which he could do something practical to help, he did it. Those times, and there were many of them, when the practicalities of my care were in the hands of consultants, he took the time to discuss my treatment, and answer my worries and concerns about it. Dr. Murray recognised that my pain not only affected me, but had numerous ramifications, and he took time to talk them through. On other occasions, when nothing could be done, he listened, or was quiet, as I needed. He had the gift of being appropriate.

That kind of medicine is time consuming, but it soothes away hurts that no prescription can heal. It also provides a safety valve for the patient, and so is most effective preventive care. Some time ago it seemed that my condition was not going to change radically, I discussed this with him, and we talked about the support I would need in the absence of medication giving effective pain relief. It concerned me that my consultations with him were using a disproportionate amount of his time. His reply was that he could write a prescription every three minutes, and that if a patient wanted that kind of care they could go to another doctor. The kind of medicine which he practised took more time. His patients had to be prepared to wait for it, knowing that each would get the time they needed when they saw him.

I was so grateful to Dr Murray when another relationship did not work out. Pain is subjective, trying to describe it is frustrating. Meeting someone who, although he never denied the fact of my pain, seemed to imply that perhaps it was not so bad as I was making out, was very hard indeed. That was the situation I was in with the consultant who took on my care. Because he perceived pain as a symptom rather than being a problem in itself, he was unable to support and help me. Having said that, he did, after much asking, refer me to a consultant in pain relief. I am thankful to him for that. Our meetings were never less than professionally correct, but they did at times become awkward and embarrassing. There was no potential for a therapeutic relationship between us. After a while, and a lot of thought and prayer, I requested to be transferred into the care of another doctor. This was done with no unpleasantness, and probably as much to his relief as to mine!

I was hesitant when I first went to meet the professor who took over my case a year after my accident. It concerned me that he might think of me as a trouble-maker because I had asked to be changed from my previous consultant. The facts were so different from the fears. He was kind,

MY COMPANIONS

helpful and understanding right from the first
consultation. Over the time I was his patient he
sought out every way of helping, and referred me
to other specialists where his expertise ended.
He made himself available in such a way that, if I
had a problem, I could phone and ask to see him
rather than wait for my next appointment. In a
busy city hospital that does not often happen.

A real breakthrough came as a result of attending the Pain Relief Clinic. Of course the consultant there knew what physical condition caused
the pain I was suffering. But he also recognised
that pain, in itself, was a real problem. Dr Murray
had all along acknowledged that to be the case,
but to find someone else who appreciated it, and
used it as the basis of his treatment, was enormously relieving. During the years I attended the
clinic, the pain relief consultant tried a number
of methods of pain control. Some of these were
unpleasant, but it was a mark of the nature of the
man that he said, on one occasion when a
procedure was going to be uncomfortable, that
he would 'talk me through it.' He did. The
treatments? They have varied in their efficacy, but
none had a lasting effect.

I do not count that as failure. It seems to me
that medicine has little place for success and
failure. If we think in these terms, all medicine
ultimately fails, because every man dies. The
consultant in the Pain Relief Clinic had succeeded vastly, not in permanently removing my
pain, but in giving short-term respite, and in
supporting me through the trauma.

PAIN, MY COMPANION

Reference has already been made to my time in the rehabilitation hospital, and to the benefit I gained from that. My first meeting with the consultant in rehabilitation medicine was full of surprises! He chatted pleasantly for a little while, then got behind my 'I'm coping' face to my 'I'm hurting' heart. He talked about distress. I had expected him to discuss pain. He asked if I thought Angus felt I was any less attractive as a wife because of my handicap. I thought I was the only one to harbour a doubt like that. He asked how the children coped with the embarrassment of having a disabled parent. He could certainly phrase a pertinent question! That interview hurt so much that I knew he could help.

While I was in hospital on that occasion, I was in the care of a Christian senior registrar. That was a rich experience, because he was able to meet my needs at a profound level. I found it easy to share my cares and concerns with him. I did not feel any temptation to pretend. For a Christian to have a doctor who is of the same mind is of enormous benefit. This is particularly true when a problem is long-term or severe because it enables the working out of thoughts and reactions within a relationship in which the foundation of the patient's viewpoint is understood. I will long treasure the memory of the times I spent with that particular brother in the Lord.

The programme of treatment which I underwent involved a multi-disciplinary approach. I therefore met a whole new set of medical professionals. The psychologists, physiotherapists in the gym and in the comfort of the hydrotherapy pool, occupational therapist, and an enormously supportive nursing staff slotted their contributions into the programme and did me good. What was a particular blessing was my awareness that although all these folk had a job to do, and were doing it with me as their patient, they were still allowing me my integrity. I was still in control. Nobody had taken over.

It was a hard time, physically and emotionally. I will not deny that. But I quote again from my diary, written just the day before my discharge, 'The time here has hurt a lot ... It is the kind of hurt a child would feel when held terribly tightly to save it from a dangerous situation... but I've always been aware of the support undergirding the whole programme.' I will add to that – I was never unaware that the professionals involved were people, and they on no occasion denied my personhood. All the treatments I had were by negotiation. I was made to feel part of the team which was managing my problem. After all, the pain is mine, it should not be otherwise.

For some months after that period in hospital I attended as an out-patient two or three times each week. Progress was slow, but there was progress. Hydrotherapy gave temporary, but nonetheless welcome, respite from pain, and the entertainment value of the hydrotherapy pool was much appreciated welcome! After six months I still needed crutches to walk but I could walk further, faster and less painfully.

PAIN, MY COMPANION

Towards the end of 1988 it became clear that I had gone as far as I probably would go. The doctors who were caring for me felt that the time had come for me to know that. What they told me was not news. I had already realised that I would probably not walk again without support, and that pain as a companion had come to stay. I was grateful for their honesty and their sensitivity. It can be no easy thing to give that kind of prognosis to a patient even when you are almost sure that she knows it already.

What might have been the start of a bad patch, God used as an opening and a new beginning. My pain relief consultant mentioned that acupuncture might give some ease. He suggested that I try it. I was more than willing to experiment with drug-free therapies. Dr. Stevenson, my acupuncturist, was refreshing to meet. He has a profound understanding of what pain and hurt do to a person and was therefore enormously helpful at that level. But even more help was to come. With only a few needles in place for a short time, acupuncture produced pain relief as effective as any of the drugs I had been taking. The treatment needed to be repeated daily so he taught me where and how to put in the needles. The first night I used them before going to bed I enjoyed a few hours of natural sleep. Those simple words can in no way convey the blessing of sleep after many months of sleeplessness. On a visit to Alison's school some time later, Angus discovered a story she had written about me pinned on the wall. In it she described my problem and said that I had some special needles I put in myself to help it. We wondered what other parents who read that must have thought!

Alongside acupuncture Dr Stevenson taught Autogenic Relaxation. I had discovered that relaxation could help reduce pain when I was in the rehabilitation hospital. Since then I had used a cassette which went through a process of reducing tension and found it beneficial. It seemed wise to attend a course in Autogenic Relaxation and to gain whatever further benefit that could give. The positive results of that technique were needed for the next chapter which God was about to unfold.

A little while after beginning acupuncture treatment Dr Stevenson showed me an article about work being done in London on my very specific problem. When I read it I discovered words I had looked for and not found, words to describe the sensations I had been experiencing. I asked my professor for a referral to the consultant in London, and within a few weeks, in this age of long waiting lists and complaints about the National Health Service, I was in hospital as his patient.

The treatment there was vastly interesting but potentially quite painful. The course in Autogenic Relaxation enabled me to cut myself off from much of the pain and even to find the experience at times pleasurable. The doctor who was doing my treatment realised that, and suggested that the clinical psychologist might be able to help 'fix' in my mind, using self-hypnosis, the feeling of pain-freedom which I had for a time after each treatment. I was a little shy of that suggestion because I thought that hypnosis would involve another person taking over my mind! However, after talking it over with the clinical psychologist — a Scots girl, and welcome she was too while I was in the south of England — I realised that that was not the case. The results were startling. I was in hospital for a month, and by the time I was discharged I had had the benefits of the drug therapy and the resultant periods of total pain relief. Even when the drug's most immediate effects had worn off I was in less pain than I had been before. I had also been taught to use self-hypnosis to produce pain freedom by mimicking the effects of the drug therapy I had undergone.

Where does that leave me now? I have lost some of the pain I had. I can walk more comfortably although still with crutches because of a spasmodic pain problem which I cannot control. I use self-hypnosis for pain relief, especially when I know I have to stand or walk. I use it routinely before cooking or shopping, when I know the children are about to come home from school, or when I need to be able to concentrate particularly on doing something. I have a 15 — 20 minute session of Autogenic Relaxation three times each day. Its benefits I can only describe as smoothing away the jagged edge of pain with calmness. Just before going to bed I use acupuncture to relieve pain and enable me to have some sleep. This may sound very complicated and time-consuming, but the benefits far outweigh the effort involved. Three years ago pain had such control of me that I was addicted to Methadone. I do still carry pain-relieving tablets in my handbag, but I am now more likely to take one for a very occasional headache than for the nerve pain in my ankle.

When I review these last years, some things stand out as being of great worth. Most importantly, God has been good. He has used real problems to produce real blessings. He has changed difficulties into challenges. He is committed to my care, I have Scripture's assurance for that, and he is faithful who has made that promise.

I have a refreshing and new view of the family, immediate and extended. I loved them dearly before, of course I did, but I have found out something more of what they are made of, and I have not been disappointed.

As I look back, friends stand out like beacons. Old friends, proving their worth again; new friends, showing their depth. The privilege of being in obvious need in a Christian congregation opened my eyes to the blessings that flow from that.

My dealings with medical professionals, in their various fields, have been humbling. That so many people, in so many places, should care so much. That vast tracts of time, a lot of money, and an ocean of practical concern have been centred on me, have been for my benefit, that makes me humbly grateful.

PAIN, MY COMPANION

All these factors help to give me confidence. My pain problem, though reduced, is still with me. The supports which help me to cope change from time to time and from place to place. But God, who knows all, and overrules everything, does not change. He is the same in all the yesterdays of joy and laughter, of pain and suffering; in today, in its bustle and busyness; and in every tomorrow, to transform my uncertainties, doubts and fears by yet more demonstrations of his sovereign power.

Chapter 7

PAIN – A THEOLOGICAL PROBLEM

'With mercy and with judgement
My web of time he wove,
And aye the dews of sorrow
Were lustred by his love.'
                              Mrs Cousin

The pain that any one person bears is only a drop in the ocean of the suffering of humankind. Therefore the theological questions which that one man asks can be asked by every man who has ever felt. He too has suffered. But we can only ask theological questions of God. Only if we have faith, or at least an open mind about the existence of God, have we any right to ask theological questions at all. If not to God, to whom do we address our questions?

Day by day on the radio and television and through the press we are bombarded by the theological problem of human suffering. In one news bulletin we might hear of fighting in the Middle East, of drought conditions in an African state, and of flooding in an Indian one. To the modern mind these large-scale disasters are a source of sadness and perhaps a spur to generosity. But modern man says that there is no god, therefore there is no ultimate meaning. Life is chance and random. He has no need to explain suffering. His role is to alleviate it. There being no god, he sees no higher determining factor than nature, and nature is fickle. He will aim to

111

tame nature, and human nature, where he can. He will predict it and cope with it where he cannot.

Modern man looks at the news and feels profound sadness and compassion. He is generous as a result, but he is not confused. If life has no ultimate meaning he has no need to look for it. If he sees no benevolent force in control then he has no expectation of peace rather than war. If he conceives of no generous ruler of the cosmos then he has no reason to look for plenty rather than famine. If he believes that there is no god holding the universe in his hands then he has no reason to expect rain and sun in their seasons and a harvest to follow. Modern man believes there is no god. He has much to cause him joy, much to cause him sorrow, much to inspire him to acts of generosity and altruism, but he has no reason to be confused.

The Christian watches the same news bulletin. He hears of the war in the Middle East and he remembers that Jesus was born there. Jesus walked where the bombs are falling. Jesus died within hearing range of the gun-shots. He remembers that Jesus is the Prince of Peace... and wonders.

The newscaster changes and scenes of untold human misery appear. There is a picture of children with distended stomachs. He sees mothers starved until their bony bodies no longer even provide a comfortable last resting place for their dying babies. The Christian remembers God's promise of seedtime and harvest... and wonders.

Again the scene changes. The Christian listens to a report of a child abused by his parents – not in Africa nor in India – but closer this time, too near home. He remembers reading that Jesus gathered little children into his arms and blessed them... and wonders.

Our Christian friend listens to the end of the news and then gets up to switch off the set. He finds it difficult. He has multiple sclerosis. He is grateful for his periods of remission, he 'manages wonderfully well'. But he remembers that his body is the temple of the living God... and wonders.

The Christian looks at life and is filled with questions, but he does not have all the answers. Faith requires that the believer asks questions. The Christian who believes in a holy God looks at evil, and asks why. The man who has faith in a loving God sees hatred, and asks why. The believer knows that God is personally involved with each of his people. He feels pain, and wonders why.

As a Christian I am blessed. Although I have lots of questions, and I do not have all the answers, what I do have is the Bible. I have the source book of the whole created order. I have the Word of God the Creator. In my hand I hold the infallible, the inspired, the definitive Word of God for all men and for all time.

My pain sent me to my Bible. At first it drove me there for comfort, consolation and assurance. Some passages shone for me. Psalm 43, especially verse 5, spoke to my need — 'Why are you downcast, O my soul? Why so disturbed within me? Put your hope in God, for I will yet praise him, my Saviour and my God.' I want to put a line of exclamation marks after it!

The first few verses of Isaiah 43 spoke specifically to my pain and spoke directly to my heart. Read them slowly and savour them. 'But now, this is what the Lord says — He who created you, O Jacob, he who formed you, O Israel: 'Fear not, for I have redeemed you; I have summoned you by name; you are mine. When you pass through the waters, I will be with you; and when you pass through the rivers, they will not sweep over you. When you walk through the fire, you will not be burned; the flames will not set you ablaze. For I am the Lord, your God, the Holy One of Israel, your Saviour.'

In the first weeks after my nerve was damaged, when the pain was most acute, I found real blessing in a slim volume of psalm portions which were accompanied by photographs of the Holy Land. The degree of pain I had affected my concentration to quite a marked degree. Consequently, books which might have been very helpful were unavailable to me. My intellect longed to delve for answers, but my mind was befuddled. God knew my need, and he was fully aware of my limitations. He fed me, like a child, from his Word. One day a card would come with a verse, just the right verse. Another day my minister would call and share some Scripture truths with me.

PAIN — A THEOLOGICAL PROBLEM

For three months I was unable to go to church but during that time sermon tapes were much blessed to me. What amazed me then, and still does, is that God did not speak at random. God is the God of order not of confusion. Even in that very difficult time of pain and exhaustion God spoke to my needs: I needed comfort, and assurance. Most of all I needed to know that, even though my world had been turned upside down and inside out, God was sovereign, and totally in control.

After a time of acute pain a cocktail of drugs was worked out which went some way to meeting the problem. This was an enormous physical and mental relief. Until then I had no idea how much my mind was affected by my body. But the relative ease of body I found at this time freed my mind. I was able to begin to consider the theological problem I had encountered.

I was lent books by Christian friends which broached the subject. I sought out others. I reread volumes I had found helpful previously in this connection. I delved into the book of suffering — the Book of Job. I was asking no new question. Job and myriads of others have asked it before me, 'Why do men suffer?' I did not find myself asking the more personal question — 'Why me?' In this pain-racked and care-worn world 'Why not me?' would be more appropriate. But why suffering? Why pain? Why?

We have three constants in our consideration of the subject of suffering. We have the constants of man, of pain and of God. But where do we

115

start?

Every man is different. No two people have exactly the same life-style. No two have committed exactly the same catalogue of sins. So, although man is a constant factor in the puzzle, men's situations are so varied that perhaps we should start by considering either pain or God.

But pain is, in that respect, like man. Each person's pain is different from that of anyone else. My headache is different from your back pain. My headache today is even different from the headache I had last week. Not only do we experience pain in different degrees but our mind-set determines that we should feel the same pain differently on separate occasions. Pain is as variable as people.

Should we then start by considering our third constant – God? Is he, like man and pain, variable? No, here we have a constant who is The Constant. God's Word assures us of that: in James 1:17 (AV) we are told 'Every good gift and every perfect gift is from above, and cometh down from the Father of lights, WITH WHOM THERE IS NO VARIABLENESS, NEITHER SHADOW OF TURNING.' We read, in Hebrews 13:8, of God's Son, 'Jesus Christ is the SAME, YESTERDAY, AND TODAY, AND FOR EVER.' Here we find the truly constant. Let us start looking at the puzzle of why God allows pain, by first looking at God.

What is God? Is that a question we can begin to try to answer? God is the great 'given' of Scripture. The Bible nowhere defines God. The

116

Bible assumes God. Genesis 1:1 – 'In the beginning, God...' A god who could be defined would
not be a god worth worshipping. He would
be merely as high as the highest conceivable
thought of the human intellect, as deep as the
profoundest depth of human emotion, and as
powerful as the strongest creature. He would be
a god in the shape of man. He would be man at
his best, but man at best.

Scripture, while it does not define God, does
describe him. The descriptions of God and of his
nature which we have in Scripture are divine
self-revelations. The sum of them all is God's
total revelation of himself to his creatures. Let us
then look at the characteristics which the Bible
attributes to God. In doing this we must remember that God is not merely the aggregate of all his
revealed attributes but that they are expressions
of his Being in action.

God is eternal.
Psalm 102:25–27: 'In the beginning you laid the
foundations of the earth, and the heavens are the
work of your hands. They will perish, but you
remain; they will all wear out like a garment. Like
clothing you will change them and they will be
discarded. But you remain the same, and your
years will never end.' Deuteronomy 33:27: 'The
eternal God is your refuge, and underneath are
the everlasting arms.' Man's life is short. His day
lasts for but a moment on the face of time. But
God is for ever. Before matter was, God was. And
God will be into the infinitude of foreverness.

Revelation 22:13: 'I am the Alpha and the Omega, the First and the Last, the Beginning and the End.' He is unceasingly 'I AM' — not 'I was not, then I was, now I am, then I will be, then I will cease to be.' God for ever, and ever and ever, without end.

God is omnipresent.

Psalm 139:7–12: 'Where can I go from your Spirit? Where can I flee from your presence? If I go up to the heavens, you are there; if I make my bed in the depths, you are there. If I rise on the wings of the dawn, if I settle on the far side of the sea, even there your hand will guide me, your right hand will hold me fast. If I say, "Surely the darkness will hide me and the light become night around me," even the darkness will not be dark to you; the night will shine like the day, for darkness is as light to you.' We read of God's presence in his created world right throughout Scripture. God walked with the first man. Genesis 3:8 says: 'The man and his wife heard the sound of the Lord God as he was walking in the garden in the cool of the day.' He was with his people throughout the long history of the children of Israel. Psalm 145:18: 'The Lord is near to all those who call on him.' He was present with mankind in the Person of Christ. As we are reminded in John 1:9–10: 'The true light that gives light to every man was coming into the world. He was in the world, and though the world was made through him, the world did not recognise him.' And he promises to remain present with his people always. Matthew 28:20: 'Surely I am with you always, to the very end of the age.'

God is all-powerful.

'Yours, O Lord, is the greatness and the power and the glory and the majesty and the splendour, for everything in heaven and earth is yours' (1 Chron. 29:11). Our God is so powerful that he rules the very elements. 'By his power he churned up the sea' (Job 26:12) and Christ, by his power, stilled the tempest. Psalm 150:1–2 shouts aloud about the power of God 'Praise the Lord. Praise God in his sanctuary; praise him in the mighty heavens. Praise him for his acts of power; praise him for his surpassing greatness.' Not only is God powerful, God is all-powerful. All human power derives from God. 'There is no authority except that which God has established' (Rom. 13:1). The creation came into being by the power of God. All power in the creation is answerable to God. At the end of all ages the hosts of heaven will ascribe all power to Almighty God. In Revelation 7:12 we have the song of angels: 'Amen! Praise and glory and wisdom and thanks and honour and power and strength be to our God for ever and ever. Amen!'

God is holy.

To be holy means to be different, to be set apart. The God of the Bible is holy. He is totally different. He is completely 'other'. Everything to do with him is different. The very ground on which he was, when he addressed Moses, was different. God said, 'Take off your sandals, for the place where you are standing is holy ground' (Ex. 3:5). God's day, the sabbath is different. 'The Lord commanded, "Tomorrow is to be a day of rest, a holy Sabbath to the Lord"' (Ex. 16:23). The holiness of God is quite beyond our imaginings because we have nothing which which to relate the concept. Of God's power and his presence we can begin to conceive. We understand human power and what is meant by human presence. But we cannot even attain to the foothills of the concept of God's holiness, God's 'otherness'. At that mystery we can only wonder.

God is righteous.
How do we define the righteousness of God? Scripture shows us that God's righteousness finds its expression in his covenant relationship to his people, and in his unswerving commitment to keep that covenant. God's covenant-keeping is the establishment of his own righteousness. In Genesis 17:7 we have this covenant. God said to Abraham, 'I will establish my covenant as an everlasting covenant between me and you and your descendants after you for the generations to come, to be your God and the God of your descendants after you.' The terms of the covenant are everlasting. The righteousness of God is the measure of the perfection with which he has kept that covenant. The covenant

has been broken on the side of man time without number, but God is faithful. God is righteous. God's righteousness in his covenant-keeping has three implications for us:

(1). If the covenant is broken by man, God's righteousness requires justice. 'Righteousness and justice are the foundation of your throne; love and faithfulness go before you' (Ps. 89:14). In Jeremiah 23:5–6 we read of the justice and righteousness of Christ, who is the seed of Abraham. God said, 'I will raise up to David a righteous Branch, a King who will reign wisely and do what is just and right in the land. In his days Judah will be saved and Israel will live in safety. This is the name by which he will be called: The Lord Our Righteousness.' Here we see God's righteousness and justice hand in hand in the context, again, of the outworking of the Abrahamic covenant.

(2). Just as God's righteousness provides a backdrop for his justice, so it does for his wrath. A covenant is made to be kept by both parties equally. God has remained faithful to his covenant with Abraham but man has not. Scripture teaches us that God is justly wrathful. The anger of God is integral to both the Old and New Testament. In Jeremiah 21:12 we read of God saying, 'Administer justice every morning; rescue from the hands of the oppressor the one who has been robbed, or my wrath will burn like fire because of the evil you have done – burn with no-one to quench it.' In the New Testament, we read of the Lord Jesus being wrathful in response to inhumanity, Jesus 'looked round at them in anger' (Mark 3:5). God's wrath results from his righteousness.

(3). God's righteousness and his justice go hand-in-hand, but joining with them in a glorious trio is God's mercy. If God were not righteous, he could not be merciful. If God were not righteous he would not have eternally kept the covenant. And if that were the case he would have no cause for wrath against mankind who has broken it. But we have a God to whom Habakkuk could say, 'Lord, I have heard of your fame; I stand in awe of your deeds, O Lord. Renew them in your day, in our time make them known; IN WRATH REMEMBER MERCY' (Hab. 3:2). No wonder Habakkuk went on to say in the following verses, 'His glory covered the heavens and his praise filled the earth. His splendour was like the sunrise; rays flashed from his hand, where his power was hidden.' Hallelujah!

God is gracious.
As Psalm 86:15 says: 'You, O Lord, are a compassionate and gracious God, slow to anger and abounding in love and faithfulness.' In Scripture we discover that God's grace has two forms. In his COMMON grace he deals with all men, believer and non-believer alike. 'He causes his sun to rise on the evil and the good, and sends rain on the righteous and the unrighteous' (Matt. 5:45). When we look around us we see that health, wealth, talents and blessings are distributed throughout mankind without regard to

their response to the gospel. God deals graciously with all men. But our God is also a God of SAVING grace. His saving grace is his total loyalty to his covenant and to his covenant people. He will not break his covenant. He will not let his people go. Jesus said of his sheep, 'I give them eternal life, and they shall never perish; no-one can snatch them out of my hand. My Father, who has given them to me, is greater than all; no one can snatch them out of the Father's hand. I and the Father are one' (John 10:28–30). Herein is the basis of the Christian's assurance.

God is love.

Is there an attribute of God better known than this? Folk who will not countenance a holy God, or a righteous God, will glibly talk about a loving God. Love seems to be the highest point of human imaginings. But because man sees it in the light of human love, therefore love tainted by sin, he subconsciously perhaps reckons that a loving God will not be a severe God, or a judgemental God. It is assumed that a loving God will love sinners enough to 'let them off'. But God's love is a reflection of his totality. We read in 1 John 4:8 that 'God is love,' but God is not only loving in an abstract way, he loves in action. 'This is how God showed his love among us: he sent his one and only Son into the world that we might live through him' (1 John 4:9). Probably the best-known verse in Scripture is a description of the active love of God. 'For God so loved the world that he gave his one and only Son, that whoever believes in him should not perish but have eternal life' (John 3:16). God is committed to love and he is faithful.

We started our consideration of God by discovering that he was constant and without variableness. But God is not unlimited. God is limited by the dictates of his own nature. He cannot therefore be an absent God, because he is omnipresent. Nor can he be a weak God, because he is all-powerful. God cannot cease to be God or become less than God, because he is eternally everything he is. God is immutable.

The second factor in our puzzle — why does God allow man to suffer? — is man. Let us now consider what Scripture says about him.

In Genesis 1:26 we learn something about man even before he was created. We are in fact given a view of the master plan of the Creator! God said, 'Let us make man in our image, in our likeness, and let them rule over the fish of the sea and the birds of the air, over the livestock, over all the earth, and over all the creatures that move along the ground.' We read on and find that God made man according to his plan for him. He then made man aware of his purpose for mankind. 'So God created man in his own image, in the image of God he created him; male and female he created them. God blessed them and said to them, "Be fruitful and increase in number, fill the earth and subdue it. Rule over the fish of the sea and the birds of the air and over every living creature that moves on the ground"'(Gen. 1:27).

PAIN — A THEOLOGICAL PROBLEM

At the end of the days of creation God viewed the work of his hands. 'God saw all that he had made, and it was very good' (Gen. 1:31). If we think back to the attributes of God we must conclude then that there were no flaws in the created order. God would not have been satisfied with other than the perfect. So man was created flawless, perfect. He was without any deviation from the plan which God had conceived.

Where does pain fit into this? Did God's perfect creation include suffering? We must search on in the Scriptures for an answer to this. In Genesis 3 we have the narrative of the Fall. God allowed Adam and Eve to eat of any of the trees in the garden of delights in which he had placed them — except one. God said, 'You must not eat from the tree of the knowledge of good and evil, for when you eat of it you will surely die' (Gen. 2:17). We learn three things from this verse. Firstly, man had no knowledge of good and evil. He was living in the perfection of God's creation. Secondly, man had the facility for choice. God instructed him not to choose to eat of that particular tree, therefore God had made man with the freedom to exert will. And thirdly, death was not part of the perfection of the created order. Death would only enter if man chose to eat of the forbidden fruit, to disobey the Maker's instructions, to rebel.

The narrative goes on and records that rebellion. How, tempted by Satan, Eve ate. Persuaded by Eve, Adam also ate the forbidden fruit.

They found God's word to be true. They gained the knowledge of good and evil and made use of that knowledge right away. Adam tried to pass the buck to Eve, and Eve to Satan — they sinned. They also looked at themselves, the pinnacles of God's creation, and saw a need for shame. They covered themselves from the sight of God and from the view of each other. They sinned. There followed the most awful confrontation of all time. God walked in the garden to enjoy fellowship with Adam and Eve and met with half-clothed, shamefaced, fearful and sinful humanity. Scripture gives us the record of God's dealings with his fallen creatures. We find there the first mention of pain.

Here we have a most important clue in our search for an answer to the question of suffering mankind. God said to Eve, 'I will greatly increase your pains in childbearing; with pain you will give birth to children' (Gen. 3:16). But pain was not going to be the experience of woman only, the first sinner. God also addressed himself to Adam, 'Cursed be the ground because of you; through painful toil you will eat of it all the days of your life... By the sweat of your brow you will eat your food until you return to the ground, since from it you were taken; for dust you are and to dust you will return' (Gen. 3:17,19). Adam and Eve disobeyed God. They rebelled against their Creator. They sinned. And in so doing they introduced into God's perfect creation pain, suffering and death.

God had made man out of the dust of the

ground (Gen. 2:7); now, because of sin, to that dust he would return. His life would be tainted by suffering. His children would be borne at the cost of pain. And his days would end in death. His body would be committed to the earth and in the course of time his dust would mingle with that round about it. Such was the devastating effect of sin in the lives of Adam and Eve, and, by inheritance, in the lives of all who have ever followed. In case we should ever be in any doubt about the cause of suffering or the origin of death, God, in his Word rehearses often the salutary message. 'The wages of sin is death' (Rom. 6:23). 'Just as sin entered the world through one man, and death through sin, and in this way death came to all men, because all sinned' (Rom. 5:12).

God created man with free will, to be a free agent. He did not make an automaton, a mechanical device forever programmed to worship its Maker. Adam and Eve chose to use their freedom to rebel against God and everyone since has inherited the resultant sinful nature and has actualized it in his own life by personal sin.

We have looked at the nature of God, and we have considered the nature of man, we need search no further — we have found the nature of pain and of suffering. We started with a perplexing puzzle, we have found a deep mystery.

But there are still 'whys'? Why did God not swat Adam and Eve as a man might dispose of offending flies? Why did God not start again, make new people, rethink the pattern? Why did

127

God not ignore their sin and hope that they would not make too much a mess of his creation? Why did God not forgive their sin, pretend it never happened, and let them begin again?

To try to find some answers to these questions let us put together the facts we have gleaned from Scripture. Let us apply to man in his fallen state what we know about the nature of Almighty God.

God is eternal.
He is forever the same. God conceived of the pattern for mankind. It was perfect. It was eternally perfect. God could conceive of no better — man was patterned in his image (Gen. 1:27). Had God been less than eternal then his plan might have been less than eternally perfect. Had God been mutable, and therefore varying throughout the course of eternity, his image in which man was made might also have varied. But God is eternal, unchangeable, and therefore he could not improve upon the plan of man, man made in his own image. Freedom to will is an integral part of man's reflection of the image of God. God made man the highest point of his creation to fellowship with him. But man had to choose to do so. God could have derived no pleasure from a mechanistic worship machine.

God is omnipresent.
Is there anything in the forever presentness of God which could have altered the consequences of the Fall? Is there anything in the vigilance of a

128

parent which can always prevent a child from making a choice which will do him hurt? Only by taking over the will of a child could a parent prevent potential harm. Only by taking away the person-ness of people could the ever-present God have prevented the entrance of sin into the world. It could have been done only by transforming free mankind into a set of wind-up, clockwork toys.

God is all-powerful.
Surely if anything in the nature of God could have prevented the disaster of the Fall, his power is that characteristic. But the power of God is not independent of the rest of his nature. He could not call on his limitless power to change his perfection and so change the image of himself in which man is made. God is Unity, his nature does not war against itself.

God is holy.
We must conclude that because of the fact that we are made in the image of God, and therefore with freedom of will, the fall was possible. The fall was not inevitable. The choice might have been made not to eat of the fruit of the forbidden tree. Remember, God looked at newly created man and saw that he was good, so he did not have a fault programmed into his system. His choice of sin was made quite freely. Where does the holiness of God fit into this picture? We read in Habakkuk how it is said to God that he is so holy, so different, that 'Your eyes are too pure to

look on evil; you cannot tolerate wrong' (1:13). Such was the holiness of God in response to the fallen sinful nature of man. 'The Lord God banished him from the garden of Eden to work the ground from which he had been taken. After he drove the man out, he placed on the east side of the garden of Eden cherubim and a flaming sword flashing back and forth to guard the way to the tree of life' (Gen. 3: 23–24).

God is righteous.
The fact of God's holiness barred the way between man and God. Cherubim and a flaming sword flashed between them.

When we considered the righteousness of God we saw that it was defined in terms of the covenant he made with Abraham. In this covenant we have a magnificent and awesome breakthrough. God approached man! Sinful man could not, would not, did not want to approach God. But Almighty God could, would and did want to approach sinful man. This is a thought which pushes us beyond the very limits of faith. Can such a thing be true? Yet we read the narrative of this approach just as we read the narrative of man's rebellion. In Genesis 17 we find that God approached Abraham. He entered into a covenant relationship with him, a mere man. God's righteousness has since totally committed him to the keeping of this 'everlasting covenant ... to be your God.'

PAIN – A THEOLOGICAL PROBLEM

God is gracious.

When we think about the graciousness of God we reach towards inconceivable heights. Can it be true that God should be gracious to men who despoiled his heaven on earth, to a people who broke covenant with their God despite his unswerving faithfulness to its terms? 'You, O Lord, are a compassionate and gracious God, slow to anger, abounding in love and faithfulness' (Ps. 86:15). But the grace of God is fundamental in relation to man's sin. 'If, by the trespass of the one man, death reigned through one man, how much more will those who receive God's abundant provision of grace and of the gift of righteousness reign in life through the one man, Jesus Christ' (Rom. 5:17). God's grace is saving grace. But from what does it save? Man sinned at the fall and the world we live in still bears the fruit of that sin. We live in a war-torn, pain-racked, sin-stained, suffering society. The world though affected by the fall is, by God's common grace, still beautiful, still producing fruit. There is still laughter, love, health, and creativity. But, by God's saving grace, there is a way out of the impasse. God's saving grace resulted in an act of unspeakable love.

God is love.

God's love could not make him pretend that nothing happened at the Fall. But the love of God was not diminished by what did happen at the Fall. God continued to love erring mankind. Throughout history he worked out his love in his care for mankind. In the fulness of time, in Jesus Christ, he gave himself, out of love, for mankind. 'The wages of sin is death' and that price had to be paid. God demanded payment. And God paid the debt. 'The wages of sin is death, but the gift of God is eternal life through Christ Jesus our Lord' (Rom. 6:23). 'This is how we know what love is: Jesus Christ laid down his life for us' (1 John 3:16). The free gift of forgiveness of sins and eternal life is offered to all, even though it must be appropriated by each individually. The good news of the gospel is, 'If we confess our sins, he is faithful and just to forgive us our sins and purify us from all unrighteousness' (1 John 1:9). The price that Christ paid for our salvation was his life. This brings us full circle, back to the subject of pain and suffering, and the end of suffering, death. Man's sin resulted in the introduction of pain, suffering and death into the world. Christ's pain and suffering and death broke down the barrier in our relationship with God. That barrier was erected at the Fall and the way back to God was reopened at Calvary for all who choose to walk in it.

Our study of the nature of God and of man has given us Scripture's answers to some of our questions about why a loving God created a society in which he allows suffering. What we have found out has been in regard to mankind in general. But what about man in particular? What about the pain you are still suffering having had shingles a year ago? What about my nerve pain? Does Scripture have anything to say about the pain and suffering of particular individuals? The Book of Job records the suffering of one man. For our benefit it also opens a window into heaven to allow us to see something of the nature of Job's situation in relation to God and to Job's life-style. Had we only the Book of Genesis for our guidance we might conclude that any pain a person feels is the direct result of a specific sin which he has committed, that God meets each act of rebellion with an immediate act of judgement. Let us look at the Book of Job and see what we can discover there.

The writer of the Book of Job sets the scene for us in chapter one. There we have a description of Job and we find him to be a good man, a wealthy man, a family man and a godly man (1:1–6). Later in the same chapter we have another description – this time we find ourselves watching a confrontation and listening to a conversation between God and Satan. In the course of the conversation we discover a number of things:

(a). that Satan is answerable to God (1:6–7).

(b). that God was pleased with Job (1:8).

(c). that Satan's attack on Job was not because of personal sin but as a result of personal righteousness (1:8).

(d). that God permitted Satan's dealings with Job (1:12).

(e). that God limited the activity of Satan (1:12).

Even in this first chapter of the book we can learn much of value. Firstly, we discover something of the cosmic nature of temptation. Satan's answer to God's question regarding his activities tells us that he had been 'walking here and there, roaming round the earth' (1:7). Satan is a opportunist. He is ever amongst us looking for opportunities to incite rebellion. But Satan does not have the upper hand. He is answerable to God. The wiles of the devil are not outside of the power of God. God is, after all, Almighty God. Satan is as answerable to God for his activities as I am for mine, both on a day-to-day basis, and in terms of eternal judgement.

Secondly, Job was a good man. Even holy God recognised his righteousness and boasted of him to Satan (1:8). Job, however, was a sinner in common with all mankind. So it would seem from God's estimate of him that he was a forgiven sinner. What we can be quite clear about is that God did not use Satan to punish Job for his sins. In the eyes of God Job was a good man.

Thirdly, Satan was provoked by Job's righteousness (1:9–10). He argued that God had been so good to Job that it was worth his while to worship him. Sinfulness pleases Satan; goodness provokes him. A good life is a challenge to the tempter. A forgiven sinner is to him a ideal specimen on which to try to work out his acts of rebellion.

Fourthly, God permitted Satan's dealings with Job. God loved Job, and knew what Job was made of. After all, God had made him what he was. Satan's taunts that Job would curse God if all his blessings were taken away did not make any headway with God. He knew the heart of his servant. He knew that, should every good thing be removed, Job would not curse his Creator. The issue was never in doubt. The battle was fought in the battlefield of a man, but the outcome was always with the Lord. Satan may rant and rave, may tempt and confuse, but he is fighting an eternally losing battle.

Fifthly, God limited the activities of Satan. God knew the limit of Job's endurance and demanded that Satan remain within it. God does not change. He knows the limit of my endurance and he has promised that I will never be called upon to go beyond it. I do not know my limit, neither did Job know his, but the one who made both of us does. We must learn to couple together the two great thoughts of Scripture. 'He knows what we are made of, he remembers that we are dust' (Ps. 103:14), and, 'God keeps his promise, and he will not allow you to be tested beyond your power to remain firm; at the time you are put to the test, he will give you the strength to endure it, and to provide you with a way out' (1 Cor. 10:13).

These five Scripture truths go some way to demisting our thinking on the subject of personal pain, and all are consistent with the attributes of God which we have already considered. But we do not know the mind of God. We must leave great mysteries in his care. The mystery of human pain and suffering is safe in his hands.

There is much more we can learn from Job about living with pain and suffering but that deserves a separate chapter.

Chapter 8

JOB – A SUFFERING SAINT

'Ye must learn to swim and hold up your head
above the water,
even when the sense of his presence is not
with you to hold up your chin.'
Samuel Rutherford

We have all read books or seen films which, in
the course of the story, flash back to an event
which has taken place in the past; forward to one
still to happen; or perhaps take a sideways step
and describe a concurrent event but in quite a
different place. Something of that kind takes
place in the Book of Job.

At one level we read of the life of Job, as he
sees it, day by day. We are, however, also given
glimpses into heaven, where we read of God's
involvement in Job's circumstances. We see both
sides of a closely-woven tapestry of events. But
we must remind ourselves, over and again, that
Job did not have the privilege of the access we
are given into the mind of God. He only saw the
tangled threads of the underside of the tapestry.
We see the wonderful picture that was being
woven above.

We know a lot about Job. He was an upright
man. 'This man was blameless and upright; he
feared God and shunned evil.' He was a wealthy
man. 'He owned seven thousand sheep, three
thousand camels, five hundred yoke of oxen
and five hundred donkeys, and he had a large

number of servants.' Job was a family man. 'He had seven sons and three daughters.' 'His sons used to take turns holding feasts in their homes, and they would invite their three sisters to eat and drink with them.' And Job was also a prayerful man. 'When a period of feasting had run its course, Job would send and have his children purified. Early in the morning he would sacrifice a burnt offering for each of them, thinking, "Perhaps my children have sinned and cursed God in their hearts." This was Job's regular custom' (Job 1:1–5).

Immediately following that description of a good man we have our first glimpse into God's workings, and we learn something about Satan. We see that Satan is answerable to God. 'One day the angels came to present themselves before the Lord, and Satan also came with them. The Lord said to Satan, "Where have you come from?" Satan answered the Lord.' Satan is a servant of God's purposes. He is permitted to do his evil deeds to further the work of God. Some are willing servants of God. Some are unwilling servants of God. But ALL must serve God.

God took the initiative – He challenged the devil with the righteousness of Job. In doing this, God placed a tremendous trust in Job, the basis of which was that God knew his man. God knew what Job was made of, because he made him. God knew the limit of Job's strength, because he was the limit of Job's strength. God knew what Job was able for, because God was Job's enabling.

Satan's response to God's challenge was contemptuous. It had been easy for Job, he claimed, he had all he wanted. He was healthy, he was wealthy. It paid him to be good, because God had been good to him.

TRY HIM, taunted God, try him. This is frightening. Within God-determined limits Satan was permitted to attack Job. The limits were clearly defined. 'The Lord said to Satan, "Very well, then, everything he has is in your hands, but on the man himself do not lay a finger."' But, although the limits were well defined, we discover in the following passage that they were devastatingly wide.

A family party was in progress when a message came of a fatal attack on Job's herds and stockmen: 'The Sabeans attacked and carried (the oxen and donkeys) off. They put the servants to the sword.' Before that messenger had left, another came with the news that a great fire had ravaged Job's flocks and servants: 'The fire of God fell from the sky and burned up the sheep and the servants.' While this man was still telling his sorry story, yet another came and told of another raid: 'Three raiding parties...swept down on your camels and carried them off. They put the servants to the sword.'

At the beginning of the book, Job was a wealthy man. In less time than it took to deliver a message, Job was poor.

Satan's work was fast and furious. But more devilish damage was yet to be done.

Before the implications of his poverty had time

to register in Job's mind, a final messenger arrived bearing the most appalling news for his master. 'Your sons and daughters were feasting and drinking wine at the oldest brother's house, when suddenly a mighty wind swept in from the desert and struck the four corners of the house. It collapsed on them and they are dead.'

At the beginning of the book, Job was a family man. In the blowing of a wind, Job was childless (Job 1:5–19).

In the midst of all this devastation, God and Satan knew that Job's safety was assured, but Job did not. YET he remained a prayerful man. 'Naked I came from my mother's womb, and naked I shall depart. The Lord gave and the Lord has taken away; may the name of the Lord be praised' (1:21). YET he remained a righteous man. 'In all this, Job did not sin by charging God with wrongdoing' (1:22).

Again we have an insight into heaven. God challenged Satan for a second time with the righteousness of Job. Satan still had an answer. 'Skin for skin!' Satan replied. 'A man will give all he has for his own life. But stretch out your hand and strike his flesh and bones, and he will surely curse you to your face' (2:4).

TRY HIM, God said, try him. God again clearly defined the limit, Job's life was to be spared. But within that limit Satan had a free hand. He wasted no time, he immediately afflicted Job with some awful boil-producing condition. Job's whole body was so inflamed and distressed that he took a piece of pottery with which to scratch himself.

Picture Job now, poor, childless, sitting on the ash-tip covered with putrifying sores, whose pain was driving him to distraction. His wife came to him with advice, 'Curse God and die!' (2:9). Did Job curse God? Did the thought of the relief that death would bring drive him to that? No, Job saw his wife's advice for what it was, foolishness. He reminded her that their riches had come from God, their poverty came also at his hand.

Remember again, we know that Job's life was not in danger, but he had no way of knowing that his awful condition was not a symptom of some life-threatening disease.

Job's friends saw all his misfortunes. We read of three of them, Eliphaz, Bildad and Zophar. They came to Job, 'to mourn with him and to comfort him' (2:11). They were deeply moved by his condition which by now had rendered him sorely changed. 'When they saw him from a distance, they could hardly recognise him; and they began to weep aloud' (2:12). They were overwhelmed by Job's tragedy, so much so that they joined him on the ash-heap and sat for seven long days in silence.

At the end of that week, Job broke the painful silence. When he did, we discover that Satan had also launched an attack on the mind of the man. Job wished he had never been born. 'May the day of my birth perish, and the night it was said, "A boy is born."' (3:3). In many ways Job's situation here reminds us of Elijah. Job and Elijah

fought great battles, Job against loss and disease;
Elijah against the prophets of Baal on Mt. Carmel.
In the aftermath of these two great victories,
Satan attacked the minds of these godly men.
Elijah asked God to take away his life. '"I have
had enough, Lord," he said, "Take my life"' (1
Kings 19:4). Job did the same. He identified with
'those who long for death...who are filled with
gladness and rejoice when they reach the grave'
(3:21–22).

In response to Job's heartfelt cry, his friend
Eliphaz spoke. He delivered his long discourse in
order to show Job that all suffering had resulted
from sin. Much of what he said is true. 'Blessed is
the man whom God corrects; do not despise the
discipline of the Almighty' (5:17). Some was
dreadfully wrong. 'Consider now: Who, being
upright, has ever perished? When were the upright ever destroyed?' (4:7). The message Eliphaz
had for Job was horrendous. 'You have lost your
wealth, Job,' he said; 'your family have been
killed. You have become dreadfully ill, Job, and
it is all your fault...' Where did Eliphaz derive his
authority for this pronouncement? His authority
was based on some kind of spiritualistic experience, the author of which he could not even
identify. 'A spirit glided past my face, and the
hair on my body stood on end. It stopped, but I
could not tell what it was. A form stood before
my eyes, and I heard a hushed voice' (4:15–16).
May God preserve us from all advice based on no
firmer foundation than that!

Poor Job. He was a deeply spiritual man,

struggling against terrific trials, and he was advised by arrogant fools who treated him as the world's worst backslider. Job was in the depths of despair. 'Oh, that I might have my request, that God would grant me what I hope for, that God would be willing to crush me, to let loose his hand and cut me off!' He was cross with Eliphaz and complained, 'A despairing man should have the devotion of his friends, even though he forsakes the fear of the Almighty. But my brothers are as undependable as intermittent streams' (6:14–15). He accused them of being like streams which look refreshing and turned out to be running with bitter water. Job needed the cool refreshment of godly friends to help him cope with severe mercies. Eliphaz brought a bitter message – you have sinned, Job, you have brought it all on yourself.

Bildad responded to Job's outpouring of his confused heart and mind to God. He brought a cool and clinical eye to the problem. 'If you will look to God and plead with the Almighty, if you are pure and upright, even now he will rouse himself on your behalf and restore you to your rightful place' (8:6). Bildad preached theology, but not lovingly, not with understanding and with no pity.

Job answered Bildad, and confounded his theology. Bildad had said that blessings were the result of goodness, and cursings the direct result of personal sinfulness. But Job, that Old Testament saint, knew a New Testament truth. 'How can a mortal be righteous before God?' (9:3).

'Though I were innocent, I could not answer (God); I could only plead with my Judge for mercy' (9:15). Job knew that there were none righteous, no not one, not even Bildad.

The battle for Job's mind was fierce. He poured out his confusion to God and to men. George Philip describes Job as 'fighting to believe in the perfect righteousness of a sovereign God: at the same time he is looking for a God human enough to come down beside him in his need.' We are blessed more that Job. We have such a one in Jesus. Job fought on — the persistence of his fight being indicative of his faith. Had the man lost his faith, he would have retreated from the battle. Satan would have reigned victorious.

Zophar contributed his piece. There was much of truth in what Zophar said, 'Can you fathom the mysteries of God? Can you probe the limits of the Almighty?' (11:7). But, in his discourse, there was no humanity. Job did not need a friend like Zophar.

Eliphaz, Bildad and Zophar, these three with all their theology and all their arrogance were of less than no help to the suffering saint. Job summed up their contributions well, 'If only you would be altogether silent. For you, that would be wisdom' (13:5). Their fine speeches were foolishness. Only their silence would have proved wise.

Despite that plea from Job for peace, the sequence of speeches and answers continued. The three so-called friends became less sympathetic at every turn, and all to the sorrow of Job's soul. Job said, 'I have heard many things like these; miserable comforters are you all! Will your long-winded speeches never end? What ails you that you keep on arguing?' 'Men open their mouths to jeer at me; they strike their cheek in scorn and unite together against me' (16:2–3,10).

Through battles of anger, of confusion, of distress and of despair, Job fought on until, in the end, Satan's wiles were confounded. From the ash-heap there blossomed a triumph of faith. 'I am nothing but skin and bones; I have escaped by only the skin of my teeth.' But, 'I know that my Redeemer lives, and that in the end he will stand upon the earth. And after my skin has been destroyed, yet in my flesh I will see God. I myself will see him with my own eyes – I, and not another. How my heart yearns within me' (19:20, 25–27). That affirmation of belief has reverberated through every century since.

Job's faith was fed and rewarded. In the closing chapters of the book we see that his confidence in God's mercy was renewed. He was given a fresh understanding of true wisdom after all the false wisdom of his friends. 'The fear of the Lord – that is wisdom, and to shun evil is understanding' (28:28).

At long and weary last, Job's three companions were silenced but not because of compassion or because they had reached agreement. They were silenced by Job's apparent unreasonableness, his intransigence, his total inability to see their points of view.

But Job was to be the victim of one last and long tirade, this time from the young man Elihu. Elihu delivered himself of a long sermon which extolled himself much, and God little. Can we grasp the weariness of it all? In his conceited eloquence, Elihu would have gone on, and on, and on. But he was interrupted by God, who silenced him by speaking out of the whirlwind to Job.

The Lord did not give his suffering saint an explanation of all his trials. Rather he gave Job an insight into his almighty majesty. Job's wounds of body and mind were salved and soothed. God showered his servant with spiritual and material blessings. Satan's cruel and fruitless assaults were all for nothing.

Job's warfare was real and so is ours. There is no believer who is not physically and spiritually afflicted at some time, and to some degree. When that is our situation we may look for and find words of comfort in the Book of Job. We must recall that although Satan's attacks may be fierce and fiendish, he is active only within parameters drawn by God. May we also also remember that God has promised that no believer will ever be tested without the strength being given to endure. Like Job, we can only see what is going on upon the earth, but 'events on earth can never be explained apart from the activity of heaven' (Philip). May we remember too that when we are confused by mistaken theology from well-meaning friends, our need is to go back to the Bible and base our thinking on the Word of God.

PAIN, MY COMPANION

As believers we are persuaded 'that neither death nor life, nor angels, nor principalities, nor powers, not things present, nor things to come, nor height, nor depth, nor any other creature, shall be able to separate us from the love of God, which is in Christ Jesus our Lord' (Rom. 8:38–39 A.V.).

Chapter 9

OUR CONSTANT COMPANION

'When he leads you through the waters,
think ye not that he has a sweet, soft hand?
You know his love-grip already;
you shall be delivered, wait on.'
Samuel Rutherford

We have thought a lot about companionship, of company both positive and negative. We have considered both the warmth of friendship and the coldness of depression. We have discussed the togetherness of loving relationships and the awful apartness of the person who is companioned by loneliness. Company, it seems, is like most things in this life. It can be good or bad, healthy or unhealthy, edifying or destructive.

For the Christian, however, there is a Companion of an altogether different order. Last century it was the tradition in some households to lay an extra place at the table for every meal. Folk did this to remind themselves that there was an unseen guest at their table, that the Lord was present wherever his people were. This quaint custom is now lost in the past, but we must not lose sight of the reality of which it spoke. The company of Almighty God is not an optional extra to Christian living. We cannot choose to have him with us when we are discussing theology and leave him outside the room door when we are gossiping about our next-door neighbour. We cannot accept the fellowship of his presence when we are handing out tracts in the High Street, and lose his company when we are wasting our boss's time. He hears the conversation at the church door and also the social chat on the office telephone and in company time. He is a third person as I talk earnestly to an unbeliever of spiritual things. He is the third person when I speak sharply to my daughter for no better reason than that I have a headache.

There is a beautiful story told of a little boy and an old lady. The old lady showed the wee chap a sampler, an old embroidery, and asked him to read what it said. The boy read aloud the words, 'Thou God seest me'. The wise lady talked of the text to the young boy. She explained that God saw all his works, good and bad, and told him that he should remember that truth all his life. But, she went on, it meant something more than that. True, God saw all deeds and misdeeds, but God ever has us in his sight because he loves us so much that he cannot take his eyes off us.

We read in Scripture of this tenderness of God's love, of this absorption he has with his people. Of Jacob it is said, God 'shielded him and cared for him, he guarded him as the apple of his eye' (Deut. 32:10). The Psalmist used that same beautiful expression in Psalm 17:8. 'Keep me as the apple of your eye; hide me in the shadow of your wings.'

For the Christian, then, there is a Companion nearer than a brother. 'A man of many companions may come to ruin, but there is a friend who sticks closer than a brother' (Prov. 18:24) The believer has a Friend more tender than a mother. 'Can a mother forget the baby at her breast and have no compassion on the child she has borne? Though she may forget, I will not forget you! See, I have engraven you on the palms of my hands; your walls are ever before me' (Is. 49:15–16). He has the assurance of a relationship with Christ throughout all time. Jesus said to his disciples, 'I will be with you always, to the very end of the age' (Matt. 28:20). And the crowning glory of the Christian is the promise of the beauty of his relationship with God in this world being consummated when the church, made up of every believer from every age, will be presented to Christ as his bride. 'Hallelujah! For our Lord God Almighty reigns. Let us rejoice and be glad and give him glory! For the wedding of the Lamb has come, and his bride has made herself ready.... Blessed are those who are invited to the wedding supper of the Lamb!' (Rev. 19:6,7,9).

The concept of the church as the bride of Christ is one which our human minds can only dimly comprehend. We look around the congregations of which we are members, we look into our hearts and minds, and we know that nothing in us, or in our churches, is lovely enough for our Lord. We see ourselves dressed in the filthy rags of even our best deeds. Our hearts and minds are steeped in the squalor of even our highest thoughts.

How do we get from where we are to where we will be? And how can the Lord of Glory understand our present situation from where he is?

Revelation 19 tells us of the change that will take place in our condition to make us ready for the wedding feast. 'The wedding of the Lamb has come, and the bride has made herself ready. Fine linen, bright and clean, WAS GIVEN her to wear' (v 8). We will be provided with fine linen wedding garments for that heavenly marriage. But for the present we are going to think of the humble homespun of the Man who came to earth to seek out his bride. How woven into the warp and weft of his seamless garment is his identification with us in the fulness of our humanness.

We have three sources into which we can delve to try to understand something of our Lord's humanity. These are the prophetic passages of the Old Testament, the narrative accounts of the life and work of Jesus in the four gospels, and the teaching of the remainder of the New Testament, particularly the epistle written to the Hebrews.

Perhaps no chapter of the Bible speaks so eloquently of the humanness of the man Jesus as Isaiah 53. We should not be able to read that passage without being moved deeply. All that is described there of Jesus' experience, he underwent for us. Think of Jesus, our best-beloved, and read: 'He grew up before him like a tender shoot, like a root out of a dry ground. He had no beauty or majesty to attract us to him, nothing in

150

his appearance that we should desire him. He was despised and rejected by men, a man of sorrows, and familiar with suffering. Like one from whom men hide their faces he was despised, and we esteemed him not. Surely he took up our infirmities and carried our sorrows, yet we considered him stricken by God and afflicted. But he was pierced for our transgressions, he was crushed for our iniquities; the punishment that brought us peace was upon him, and by his wounds we are healed. All we, like sheep, have gone astray, each one of us has turned to his own way; and the Lord has laid on him the iniquity of us all. He was oppressed and afflicted, yet he did not open his mouth; he was led like a lamb to the slaughter, and as a sheep before her shearers is silent, so he did not open his mouth. By oppression and judgment he was taken away. And who can speak of his descendants? For he was cut off from the land of the living; for the transgression of my people he was stricken. He was assigned a grave with the wicked, and with the rich in his death, though he had done no violence, nor was any deceit in his mouth' (v1–9).

Let us make a brief list, from this chapter, of what our Lord endured. He, the King of Glory, lacked beauty and majesty. He was despised, rejected, sorrowful and suffering. He knew human infirmities. He was stricken and afflicted by God. Christ was pierced and crushed. He was punished and wounded. Jesus knew oppression. He suffered death. The body of the Creator of the world was committed to a grave in the world he had created.

The Lord Jesus Christ, who has promised to be with us until the end of the age, has endured, to the boundary and beyond, what it means to be fully and gloriously human. Here is a truth which is too wonderful to take in. When we are tried and tested, when we are sorely pressed by the limitations of our humanness, Jesus knows how we feel. He does not know it only because he created us. He is not the great computer programmer in the sky who understands the faults in our systems because he wrote the programme. Jesus understands because he remembers. When we are sorrowful and suffering, Jesus remembers and understands. When we know human infirmities, Christ remembers and understands. When we are crushed and wounded, the Lord remembers and understands. When we face death and the grave, the crucified Lord, the risen Saviour, he remembers and he understands.

Let us move on from the Old Testament to the gospel narrative of Christ's time on earth. It is almost unnecessary to outline the humanity of Jesus. The facts are so familiar to us. But perhaps their very familiarity can take away something of their wonder. Jesus was born of a human mother, a young peasant woman, in circumstances which by any standards were very basic. The little infant had, for his comfort, a roof over his head, strips of cloth wound around him, and an animal's trough in which to lie. He had godly parents, and so far as we know a normal upbringing in the home of a carpenter. His ministry was begun when he was 30 years old, so for well over a decade he worked with his hands in a joiner's shop. The ordinariness of it all is startling when we remember that we are thinking of the King of Glory.

We see from the gospel record that Jesus had human limitations and human needs. He experienced hunger (Matt. 4:2). He knew what it was to be tested and tried by Satan (Matt. 4:3). Jesus was tired and needed sleep (Matt. 8:24). And he felt compassion on the needy and helpless (Matt. 9:36). Jesus, when he heard of the death of his friend John, needed to get away and be alone (Matt. 14:13). He was aroused when he found the temple was like a market place and his reaction there was anger (Matt. 21:12–13). The Son of God was obedient to his Father (Luke 42:42) and in the same verse we see him in his full humanness shrinking from the horror of the cross. Jesus needed friends. As he faced the cross and the open tomb he took three of his friends into Gethsemane with him (Mark 14:32–34). A little while later he knew the feeling of being let down by these same friends as they fell asleep when he most needed them (Mark 14:37–42). In that garden Jesus knew deep distress and trouble (Mark 14:33). On the cross he knew real pain and physical anguish. When offered wine-vinegar to relieve his pain, Jesus refused it. He drank not of the sponge of wine-vinegar, but of the cup of human suffering.

Jesus' chosen designation for himself was not

the Son of God, it was the Son of Man. When he was on earth he was fully God but he was also truly man. The duality of his person did not take away from his Godness or from his humanness. Every step of his walk on earth was taken with the authority of the Creator of the world. Every day of his life was marked by human limitations.

When Jesus was wounded, he bled. When he was weary, he slept. When the Lord was lonely, he sought out friends. When the King of Glory was angry, folk around him shrank from his wrath. In Gethsemane, when faced with Calvary, Jesus felt anguished. When he paid the price of our sins on the cross, the Son of God knew what it was to be forsaken by his Father God. No cry has ever been wrung from so deep in a human heart as the cry of Jesus, 'My God, my God, why have you forsaken me?' But in the moment of dereliction, when Jesus became sin for sinners, when he knew that his Father had turned his back on him, Jesus still approached God. He approached God as Judge.

With awe we follow the gospel narrative. With wonder we take away from it two great areas of identity with Christ.

Firstly, Jesus was fully human, and gloriously human. He had the human limitations and the human potential of every created being. He had physical abilities, manual dexterity, and the whole range of emotions. But he also knew the weaknesses of human flesh, the frailties of being a real man. When we are aware of joy, love,

compassion, or pity we find it easy to know that
Jesus shared, and still shares, these feelings. It is
harder, but no less true, to realise that when we
feel hunger, or weariness, or loneliness, or
apprehension or pain, or even when Satan tries
and worries us, we also stir memories in him.
Jesus understands.

Secondly, there is a whole area of our lives of
which Jesus has no memory. He was the only
man to walk on earth who perfectly kept the law
of God, who was blameless and totally free of all
sin. He has no memory of having given in to
temptation. He cannot recall remorse or repent-
ance. In these we have no identity with our Lord.
But perhaps the strangest doctrine in the whole
of Scripture finds its place here. Why did Jesus
cry from the cross, 'My God, my God, why have
you forsaken me?' Why did God turn his back on
Jesus? Habakkuk says of God, 'Your eyes are too
pure to look on evil; you cannot tolerate wrong'
(Hab. 1:13). Although Jesus was all that was
good, although he was sinless, pure and entirely
free of any wrong, on the cross the Lord of
heaven and earth became the embodiment of
evil. He became sin. The Father could not even
look at him and had to turn his back on him.
Jesus was God-forsaken. Jesus' relationship with
God then was that of the personification of sin
meeting the Judge of all sinners. Paul puts it like
this, 'God made him (Jesus) who had no sin to be
sin for us, so that in him we might become the
righteousness of God' (2 Cor. 5:21). Jesus,
during his life on earth, knew no sin, never felt

guilt. But Jesus, on the cross, was made sin, and carried the guilt of all who believe on him.

These twin wonders reach far beyond the edges of our understanding or imagination. But what we can begin to grasp at, is that everything that is the common lot of man, save sin, Jesus remembers and understands. And that sin, which was not part of his own experience, even sin, he has dealt with.

We move on to the rest of the New Testament to discover more of the humanity of Jesus. This doctrine is nowhere spelt out with greater clarity as in the letter to the Hebrews. 'Therefore, since we have a high priest who has gone through the heavens, Jesus the Son of God, let us hold firmly to the faith we profess. For we do not have a high priest who is unable to sympathise with our weaknesses, but we have one who has been tempted in every way – yet was without sin. Let us then approach the throne of grace with confidence, so that we may receive mercy and find grace to help us in our time of need' (Heb. 4:14–16).

In these verses we have reinforced for us the idea of the Lord's identification with us in our weaknesses, in our trials and in our temptations. But we also find a consequence of that identification. Because Jesus is our high priest we can approach the throne of grace with confidence. We come to one who sympathises. We come to one who understands. We come to one who remembers. We can come confidently. In our time of need, then, we have access to the sympathy, understanding and memories of the Lord, and to his practical help. When we come we are assured that we will receive from him mercy and grace to help us.

If our need is because of human weakness — if pain, hurt, sadness, weariness — if these are our needs, Jesus remembers and understands.

If our need is for help to overcome temptation and to fight against the evil one, Jesus 'himself suffered when he was tempted, he is able to help those who are being tempted' (Heb. 2:18).

If our need is the result of sinfulness and rebellion against God, then will 'the blood of Christ, who through the eternal Spirit offered himself unblemished to God, cleanse our consciences from acts that lead to death, so that we may serve the living God!' (Heb. 9:14). Therefore, 'let us draw near to God with a sincere heart in full assurance of faith, having our hearts sprinkled to cleanse us from a guilty conscience and having our bodies washed in pure water. Let us hold unswervingly to the hope we profess, FOR HE WHO PROMISED IS FAITHFUL' (Heb. 10:22–23).

So Christ came to us, that we might go to him. At the beginning of the Bible, before the Fall, we read that God walked in the garden with Adam and Eve. They knew no pain, no guilt, no hurt, nor any distress of body or mind. When Adam and Eve sinned they were cursed with the pains of life and of death. And they were banished from the garden. In Genesis 3:24 we read that God 'drove the man out.' At the end of the last book of the Bible, we read that God and his people will again be together. In the vision John had of the eternal day, redeemed man is called back to have fellowship for ever with his God. The Spirit and the bride say, '"Come!" And let him who hears say, "Come." Whoever is thirsty, let him come; and whoever wishes, let him take of the free gift of the water of life' (Rev. 22:17). The tears which have been shed over all these eons of time will be dried, God 'will wipe every tear from their eyes. There will be no more death or mourning or crying or pain, for the old order of things has passed away' (Rev. 21:4).

Chapter 10

THE GLORIOUS END OF PAIN

'The Bride eyes not her garment,
But her dear Bridegroom's face;
I will not gaze at glory,
But on my King of Grace
Not at the crown he gifteth,
But at his pierced hand:
The Lamb is all the glory
Of Immanuel's land.'

Mrs Cousin

Much of this book has been concerned with making comparisons. We have considered positive and negative company. We have compared Christ's suffering with ours. In this last chapter we are going to make one more such comparison. We find the thought in Romans 8:18 and 21, where Paul says, 'I consider our present sufferings are not worth comparing with the glory that will be revealed in us.' Then, 'the creation itself will be liberated from its bondage to decay and brought into the glorious freedom of the children of God.'

Some years ago, when my husband's brother died, our daughters were talking about their late uncle with an acquaintance of his. Our eldest daughter, realising how upset our visitor was, told him not to cry. Uncle Adam was better now. He had his leg back and his hair had grown again. The visitor, who was a Christian, looked at our four-year-old and said wistfully, 'I wish I had your faith.'

That man had a problem. He was face to face with death, the death of a young friend, and he was struggling to understand it. Isabel was old enough to know what the Bible said about the death of a Christian, and young enough that her reaction was to believe, rather than to try to understand.

Is this the kind of faith of which Jesus spoke? 'I tell you the truth, anyone who will not receive the kingdom of God like a little child will never enter it' (Mark 10:15). Christ is not advocating childishness, but childlikeness. He is not advocating the kind of childishness which disregards problems and then rushes headlong into them. Jesus is talking of the kind of childlikeness which recognises a difficulty and places trust in someone to help.

Over the years in which my mobility has depended on using crutches, it has been the little things rather than the big things which have been most difficult to accept. Two such small things illustrate my meaning here. To walk with crutches means to have one's arms fully occupied. When I am crossing a road I cannot reach out and take the hand of a child with whom I am walking. Perhaps I do not need to take her hand, but I miss the feeling of trust which comes from walking with the hand of a little one firmly held in mine. Quite differently, on one occasion, I was standing talking to two friends who had heard traumatic news, and who were feeling upset and a little threatened by it. Although we talked and shared I could not reach out a hand and touch them, not without falling over.

There is something in the reaching out to another person which speaks of trust, and of a depth of relationship.

In our relationship with God we often suffer from the chronic independence which encourages us to struggle on in our own strength, and to keep our reaching out for the Father's hand only for dire emergencies. If only we could keep in mind the incredible truth of which Jesus spoke. 'My sheep listen to my voice; I know them and they follow me. I give them eternal life, and they shall never perish; no-one can snatch them out of my hand. My Father, who has given them to me, is greater than all; no-one can snatch them out of my Father's hand. I and the Father are one' (John 10:27–30).

Although we, in our wilfulness, may metaphorically dig our hands deep into our pockets, if we are God's children, he has us firmly and eternally in his grip. Our problems in this world may so blind us that we cannot keep sight of the wonders of the next. But that does not detract at all from the glories of heaven. As believers we know the Bible to be the Word of God. If we sinfully disbelieve some of its teachings, that does not alter its veracity one bit. Jesus asks us for childlikeness, that simple trust which holds out a hand to him, which believes what he says about this world and the next, and which accepts his Word as he has given it to us.

The childlikeness with which we were created

soured at the Fall. The intellect we were given
to delve deep into the wonders of creation,
we have used to doubt the Creator. Physical
strength, given to us to enjoy and to subdue the
earth for our use and God's glory, we have used
to dominate and destroy. The trust our first
parents were given warped when they rebelled,
and became doubt. We have inherited their
doubting natures. The dependence which was
their privilege, they overthrew for independence,
and found it to be thraldom. This thraldom is our
inheritance from them.

The message of the gospel is, however, that in
Christ we can lose the nature we inherited from
our first parents. We can receive a new nature
from him. Paul says, 'If anyone is in Christ, he is a
new creation; the old has gone, the new has
come!' (2 Cor. 5:17). As Christians we would
subscribe to this and say our 'Amen.' But what
difference does it make to us in practical terms?
We would say that it affects our souls and our
eternal destinies. This of course is true. But what
of our minds and bodies? Our intellects, soured
at the Fall, look at the world differently after our
conversion. It becomes a glory and a wonder
once again. Our bodies, used to dominate and
destroy since the Fall, we see as temples of the
living God. We have a renewed enjoyment of
physical strength and prowess to the limit of the
measure we have been given them.

What about our relationship with God, which
is so basically altered at our conversion, how is
that changed in practical terms? Sadly this is the

area in which we most often have problems. The trust, with which Adam and Eve were created, the trust which changed to doubt at the Fall, what do we do with that? It seems that we still cling to our doubts. We even approach God's Word with doubt. Did Paul really write that? Is the creation narrative really true? Did Jesus really perform miracles?

We pick up a modern science text, read it and accept every word. After all the scientist who wrote it knows what he is talking about. We take a psychology book from the library shelf, read a chapter and believe it. That psychologist is an authority on his subject. We study the Highway Code to sit our driving test, learning it with great diligence. The chaps who wrote it knew what they were talking about and our ability to drive depends on it. Just before we go to bed, we pick up a Bible, the living Word of the living God. We read a passage and wonder if it really means what it says. We wonder if it applies to us today. We wonder if it is really true. Where is the childlike trust in that approach? That was where our visitor went wrong. He wished he had the child's faith about heaven. But what he was really needing was a more childlike faith in the integrity of God and in the truth of his Word.

The disease of independence from which we all suffer also changes radically at our conversion. We are totally dependent on God for our salvation. There is nothing in us to commend us. But how does our new dependence work out in practice? So many of our problems are basically caused by our struggle to remain independent. Jesus said, 'Seek first God's kingdom and his righteousness, and all these things will be given to you as well. Therefore do not worry about tomorrow, for tomorrow will worry about itself. Each day has enough trouble of its own' (Matt. 6:33–34). Paul records what the Lord said to him, 'My grace is sufficient for you, and my power is made perfect in weakness' (2 Cor. 12:9).

How many of our cares and concerns, of our worries and troubles, are carried over from yesterday, or are brought forward from tomorrow? This is especially easy to do if we have a long-term problem. But to do this is to exert unscriptural independence. We are reassured in God's Word that his strength is sufficient for us. But to live in the light of that truth we need to lay down today's burden as we go to bed tonight. We must resist the temptation to shoulder it tomorrow morning. And we have to ignore the devil's wiles when he encourages us to worry about what will happen the day following that.

As long as we are in the world, trust and dependence will continue to be problems. Satan will try his hardest to encourage doubt and foster independence. But Satan is bound. Day by day Christians by the grace of God will win battles because, in ultimate terms, the war is over. The victory is won. Christ has conquered Satan. We are living in the era of the death throes of the devil. The outcome is in no doubt. Perhaps our day to day strivings would be eased if we could think and live with that in mind. We are earth-bound but we have a great Lord in heaven. We may be on earth for many years, but we have the promise of eternity in heaven.

At some times in our lives it is easy to remember heaven. When we have had a time of rich fellowship with fellow-believers we might find ourselves longing for that deeper communion we will enjoy in heaven. When we are in a great company of Christians and we are all singing the praises of Jesus, then we can almost feel ourselves uplifted. We find ourselves looking forward with anticipation. Sometimes when we are praying, and we know the closeness of our Lord, we yearn to bask in that nearness for ever. For some in the midst of illness, the prospect of heaven gives them warmth and assurance. Others, suffering pain of body or of mind, look forward so much to leaving behind all their weariness and to putting on heavenly bodies. These folk, at these times, have a heavenly perspective, and are living in the anticipation of the glories of eternity.

There is an expression that some folk are so heavenly-minded that they are of no earthly use. That is not the kind of mind-set which this kind of thinking produces. That is the result of fairy tales. Our God is heavenly, but his hands had the callouses which resulted from the use of a hammer and a chisel.

So how do we think of heaven? How do we live with the end-times in our minds?

Firstly, we live our lives in a way that is

glorifying to God, remembering that when the end of time comes we are answerable to him. Secondly, we maintain a perspective which reminds us that our lives on this earth are short and transient in the light of eternity. Thirdly, we allow ourselves the enjoyment of anticipation of heaven. What young couple let their engagement pass without thinking about, and longing for, their marriage?

Much of this book has been devoted to thinking how Christians who suffer pain can have that experience redeemed and so live a life which is more to God's glory. It is not easy. The struggle to do so will not end until death. But trust and dependence help to produce trust and dependence.

In our world so many of us seem to be struggling to amass more goods, to acquire more disposable things, to get bigger cars, houses in better areas, and more money to invest. Those who think about it at all will explain that it gives them security. But goods can be stolen. Disposable things are disposed of. Cars rust. Houses develop dry rot. And the stock market crashes from time to time. Security? Jesus knows our need for security. He offers us the key to the strongest box. He said, 'Do not store up for yourself treasures on earth, where moth and rust destroy, and where thieves break in and steal. But store up for yourself treasures in heaven, where moth and rust do not destroy, and where thieves do not break in and steal. For where your treasure is, there your heart will be also' (Matt. 6:19–21).

THE GLORIOUS END OF PAIN

The treasures of which Christ speaks are indestructible. One is the priceless gift of a heart at home in heaven. There is also the sparkling prospect of an eternity in the presence of God. Another is the glorious jewel of the crown of life. These treasures cannot be stolen. They do not rust or decay. They do not gain interest, because their perfection cannot be augmented. There is no uncertainty about their future because they are the promised marriage gifts to the bride of Christ, from his, and our, Heavenly Father.

The priceless treasures of heaven are described in little vignettes. Our minds, our imaginations and our credulity can take no more.

The warmth of fellowship we have on earth with God and with believers will be far surpassed in heaven. John saw this, 'I looked and there before was a great multitude that no-one could count, from every nation, tribe, people and language, standing before the throne and in front of the Lamb' (Rev. 7:9).

Songs of praise which have overwhelmed our hearts on earth will be quite drowned out by the glorious hymns of heaven. John, in his vision, 'heard what sounded like a great multitude, like the roar of rushing waters and like loud peals of thunder, shouting: "Hallelujah! For the Lord Almighty reigns. Let us rejoice and be glad and give him the glory!"' (Rev. 19:6–7).

Blessings in prayer, when we have wanted to suspend time and remain ever with the Lord, will find their fulfilment at the end of time. Revelation 7:11–12 tells us that, 'they fell down on their faces before the throne and worshipped God, saying: "Amen! Praise and glory and wisdom and thanks and honour and power and strength be to our God for ever and ever. Amen!"'

The curse which has plagued all mankind since Eve then Adam ate of the fruit of the forbidden tree will be no more. Another tree will work its blessing. John tells us of it: 'On each side of the river stood the tree of life, bearing twelve crops of fruit, yielding its fruit every month. And the leaves of the tree are for the healing of the nations. No longer will there be any curse' (Rev. 22:2–3).

All the consequences of the curse — illness, decay, pain, hurt and every disquiet of body, mind or spirit — will be taken away. God 'will wipe every tear from their eyes. There will be no more death or mourning or crying or pain, for the old order of things has passed away' (Rev. 21:4).

Night and darkness will be no more. There will not even be a need for light. 'There will be no more night. They will not need the light of a lamp or the light of the sun, for the Lord God will give them light' (Rev. 22:5). And the glorious light of the Lord will cast no shadows to chill the air.

Believers who have suffered during their lives on earth, their sufferings will end. John records a conversation in heaven. 'One of the elders asked me, "These in white robes — who are they, and where did they come from?" I answered, "Sir, you know." And he said, "These are they who have come out of the great tribulation; they have washed their robes and made them white in the blood of the Lamb. Therefore, they are before the throne of God and serve him day and night in his temple; and he who sits on the throne will spread his tent over them. Never again will they hunger; never again will they thirst. The sun will not beat upon them, nor any scorching heat. For the Lamb at the centre of the throne will be their shepherd; he will lead them to springs of living water. And God will wipe away every tear from their eyes"' (Rev. 7:13–17).

During his life on earth, Jesus wore simple homespun clothes. Glorious white robes are being prepared in heaven for all who are washed clean in the blood of the Lamb. 'For the wedding of the Lamb has come, and his bride has made herself ready. Fine linen, bright and clean, was given her to wear' (Rev. 19:7–8). At the end of time the church triumphant, made up of every believer from every age, washed in Jesus' blood, dressed in wedding garments, will at last be at one with her Best-beloved at the marriage feast of the Lamb and his bride.

'Our present sufferings are not worthy to be compared with the glory that will be revealed in us.'

MUSSELS AT MIDNIGHT

Stephen Anderson

The story of Stephen Anderson contains enough excitement and variety for two lifetimes. From dancing with the Queen to playing polo in the Egyptian desert; from a farm in Perthshire to the churches in Scotland. Stephen Anderson has been a captain in the army, a ski instructor, but above all a communicator of the gospel.

160 pp   ISBN 0 906731 933   pocket paperback

PREACHING PRIEST -
THE LIFE OF MARTIN BOOS

An interesting biography of a devoted servant of Christ.
Boos was converted in the Roman Catholic Church and
the story describes the many conflicts he had with church
authorities as he persisted in preaching the true gospel.

192 pp   ISBN 1 871676 088   pocket paperback

ALICIA

Alicia   Simpson

The personal account of Alicia Simpson. She was born into a Roman Catholic family, became a nun when she was old enough, left the convent, married a nominal Protestant but all the while was being led by God to be ready to trust in Jesus as her Saviour.

This book is suitable for every age-group between thirteen and one hundred. It is very easy to read. From Sunday School prize to Old Folks' Home, it will be useful.

64 pp   ISBN 0 906731 860   large paperback

LOVE   MINUS   ZERO

Alex   MacDonald

Is there a Christian perspective on life, death, abortion, violence, the peace movement, drugs?

Is there a Christian solution to many or all of these problems?

Love Minus Zero tackles these current issues and sets them in the context of God's love towards us. Time spent in considering the answers to such problems is time well-used. Alex MacDonald is the minister at Bon Accord Church, Rosemount Viaduct, Aberdeen where he deals with a large number of young people who are facing such problems.

160 pp   ISBN 0 906731 925   large paperback

BEHOLD YOUR GOD

Donald Macleod

The study of God has occupied minds for centuries. In this book the author asks us to forget our preconceptions and looks at the God of the Bible, to see there his greatness, power, justice and, above all, his love for human beings.

160 pp

ISBN 1 871676 096   large format hardback

ISBN 1 871676 509   large format paperback

THERE IS AN ANSWER

Leith Samuel

The book contains straightforward, yet loving answers to the real questions that face all Christians - guilt, loneliness, depression, guidance. It is a book not only for the troubled but for those who would like to help others overcome their problems.

The author is a well-known speaker and was formerly pastor of Above Bar Church, Southampton.

160 pp   ISBN 1 871676 061   pocket paperback

To Be Published In Early 1991

(1) The *Autobiography of William Still*, the well known minister of Gilcomston South Church of Scotland in Aberdeen.

(2) *The Only Way To Walk*, an inspiring account of James Brown, who despite losing both his legs in an accident, has maintained a tremendous witness to Jesus Christ both in his hometown and beyond.